Mastering Campaign Trading for Neutral and Mildly Directional Spreads

with AI Support Examples.

Tom Batchelor

Firebird Trading Systems, LLC

Disclaimer

This book is intended for informational and educational purposes only. The information presented in this book is not a substitute for professional financial or legal advice. The author and publisher make no representations or warranties of any kind, express or implied, about the completeness, accuracy, reliability, suitability or availability with respect to the book or the information, products, services or related graphics contained in the book for any purposes. Any reliance you place on such information is therefore strictly at your own risk.

The author may include affiliate links in this book. If you purchase a product or service through one of these links, the author may receive a commission. The presence of affiliate links does not affect the content, or recommendations made in this book. The author only includes affiliate for products or services that they believe will add value to the reader.

Please consult with a professional financial advisor or attorney before making any financial decisions. The author and publisher do not assume any responsibility for errors, inaccuracies, or omissions. They shall not be liable for any loss or damage of any kind, including but not limited to any direct, indirect, incidental, consequential, special or exemplary damages, arising from or in connection with the use of the book or the information contained within it

Firebird Trading Systems

Contents

PLEASE READ

TradeStation is making a special offer to those who buy this book.

Follow this QR Code to the TradeStation Offer page.

Scan me!

We hope that you enjoy trading at TradeStation!

1

Introduction to Batman and Calendar Spreads

A. Welcome and review of eBook 1

Welcome

Dear reader,

Welcome to "**Mastering Campaign Trading for Neutral and Mildly Directional Spreads**," a comprehensive guide designed to elevate your understanding and application of steady money-making strategies in options trading. Building upon the foundation laid in the first eBook, "**Campaign Trading with Complex Options Spreads**," this volume focuses specifically on mastering Batman and Calendar Spread trading. Whether you are an intermediate trader aiming to refine your strategies or an advanced trader looking for nuanced techniques and analytical methods, this book is tailored for your journey towards mastery and steady income.

1. Review of eBook 1: Campaign Trading with Complex Options Spreads

Our first foray into the realm of options trading was structured around six pivotal strategies that cater to a broad range of market conditions and trader objectives. Here's a brief recap of the strategies explored:

Bull Diagonal Strategies[1]: Introduced as a powerful tool for bullish and neutral markets, emphasizing leveraging time decay and volatility for optimal positioning.

Bear Diagonal Strategies[1]: Catered to bearish market sentiments, focusing on capitalizing from downward or neutral movements with strategic option placements.

Calendar Spreads[2]: Delved into the nuances of managing trades over different expiration periods to exploit volatility differences.

The Batman Spread[2]: A niche strategy tailored for specific market conditions, offering high flexibility and risk management potential.

The Pivot Spread[3]: Aimed at markets in transition, this strategy provides a framework for capitalizing on market pivots with manageable risk.

Gamma Scalping[3]: A dynamic approach for traders looking to actively manage positions and profit from the gamma of options.

Notes:

1. Bull and Bear Diagonal Trading is discussed in the second book of this series, "Mastering Campaign Trading with Bull and Bear Diagonal Spreads".
2. Calendar and Batman Spread Trading is discussed in this book.
3. The Pivot Spread and Gamma Scalping will be discussed in the next book in this series, which is planned for release in late 2025.

Each strategy was surveyed with an eye towards practical application, featuring case studies, risk management techniques, and adjustment mechanisms to navigate the ever-changing market landscape.

Note: Firebird Trading Systems continues to build and refine tools to support traders. **Appendix A** provides links to all **Firebird Trading Systems Products.** Our team is focused on **"Empowering Traders & Elevating Success".**

2. Focus on Calendar and Batman Spreads

With this volume, our spotlight shines on Batman and Calendar Spreads. These strategies are all about Option Theta, using a strategy that takes advantage of time decay of the short option as the primary money-making mechanism. There are times when the market is expected to remain in a range and not increase in volatility. For these times Batman and Calendar Spreads are good tools to use. Note: There are other option strategies that can be used for range bound trading environments. But Campaign Trading involves opening positions that provide possible adjustments to keep the profit potential alive for a trade, instead of ending or requiring, basically, a restart of the position.

What to Expect

In the following chapters, you'll embark on a deep dive into the world of Batman and Calendar Spreads, equipped with:

Practical Examples: Step-by-step guides on initiating positions and making adjustments based on real market scenarios.

Advanced Decision Making: A rigorous development of decision-making processes for adjustments, including studies of decision factors, including the Greeks and calculations with visual aids.

Analytical Methods: Exploration of decision trees, risk analysis, and choice optimization to enhance your strategic planning and risk assessment.

Our aim is not just to impart knowledge but to forge traders who are adept at navigating the complexities of the market with confidence and precision.

As we proceed, remember that the essence of mastering Batman and Calendar Spreads lies not only in understanding these strategies but also in honing the skill of making calculated decisions amidst the uncertainties of the financial markets. Welcome aboard this journey of discovery and mastery.

B. Overview of options trading and the significance of Batman and Calendar spreads

Options trading represents a vast and deep financial market that enables traders to leverage a diverse array of strategies to hedge, speculate, and generate income. Unlike traditional stock trading, options offer the flexibility to profit from movements in the underlying asset's price without requiring full ownership of the asset. This flexibility, combined with the use of leverage, allows for significant profit potential while managing risk. To review options trading basics prior to proceeding a **Glossary of Option Trading Terms is provided in Appendix B**.

1. The Core of Options Trading

At its core, options trading is about the strategic purchase and sale of contracts that grant the holder the right, but not the obligation, to buy (call options) or sell (put options) an underlying asset at a specified price (strike price) before a set expiration date. The beauty of options lies in their versatility, enabling traders to tailor strategies that align with their market view, risk tolerance, and financial objectives. But it does take some experience to get used to all of the possible factors involved in option price impacts.

2. Significance of Batman and Calendar Spreads

Leveraging Time and Volatility: Both Batman and Calendar Spreads uniquely position traders to exploit a market environment where stocks are not expected to trend in a specific direction. These strategies take advantage of higher premiums of short option legs (puts or calls) that are fairly close to the underlying stock price. Profits are made based on the difference in time decay between short-term and longer-term options. Batman and Calendar Spreads are typically used for neutral positions but can also be used to take advantage of some directional movement in the underlying stock. In this book Batman and Calendar Spread examples are depicted that use both puts and calls.

Risk Management: One of the key attractions of Batman and Calendar Spreads is the built-in risk management features. By carefully selecting the strike prices and expiration dates, traders can define their maximum potential loss from the outset, which is typically limited to the net premium paid for the spread plus the difference in strike prices. As you will see, Batman Spreads can be thought of as 2 separate diagonal spreads combined into a single position.

Flexibility in Adjustments: The structure of these strategies allows for adjustments based on changing market conditions or shifts in the trader's outlook. Adjustments are crucial for managing risk, protecting profits, or repositioning for anticipated market movements.

Strategic Depth: Beyond mere speculation, Batman and Calendar Spreads serve as a strategic tool for income generation and hedging. The sale of short-term options generates income that can offset the cost of the longer-term option, while the overall position can be used to hedge other holdings in a portfolio.

C. Understanding the components: longer-term options as the foundation and short-term options for income

The strategic allure of Batman and Calendar Spreads lies in the harmonious interplay between its two core components: long-term options, which form the foundation, and short-term options, which serve as a source of income. This section delves into the mechanics and rationale behind these components, illustrating how they combine to create a robust framework for trading.

1. Batman Spread Components

a. Long-term Options: The Strategy's Foundation

Long-term options, puts or calls, for Batman Spreads, are purchased with a longer expiration date and strike prices that are 10 to 20 points above and below the underlying stock price. There is no set rule about how far from the underlying stock price the long puts or calls should be purchased but remember that the choice will affect the buying power required for the position.

Key Attributes and Benefits

Capital Efficiency: Long-term options require a fraction of the capital needed to purchase the underlying asset outright, offering leverage that can amplify returns.

Time Decay Mitigation: By choosing options with longer expirations, traders can reduce the impact of time decay, preserving the option's value over a more extended period.

Volatility Exposure: Longer-term options are less sensitive to short-term price fluctuations in the underlying asset, providing a steadier position that maintains value.

b. Short-term Options: The Income Component

Conversely, short-term options, puts or calls, are sold at strike prices that are closer to the underlying stock price and have a shorter expiration date than the long options. The primary purpose of selling these options is to generate income through the premiums received, which can offset the cost of the long-term options purchased.

Key Attributes and Benefits

Income Generation: The premiums collected from selling short-term put options provide near term income, which can be used to offset the cost of the long-term calls, reduce the overall risk of the position, or be reinvested.

Time Decay Advantage: Short-term options are more heavily affected by time decay, working in the trader's favor as the seller of these options. As time passes, the value of these options diminishes, potentially leading to profitable buy-back opportunities at a lower price.

Flexibility for Adjustments: The short-term nature of these options allows traders to adjust their positions more frequently, responding to market changes or reevaluating strategies without a long-term commitment.

2. Calendar Spread Components

a. Long-term Options: The Strategy's Foundation

Long-term options for Calendar Spreads are purchased with a longer expiration date and at the same strike price as the short put. This is typically close to the price of the underlying stock. It could be above or below the underlying stock price depending on whether the trader believes that the stock price may move up or down slightly over the trading timeframe.

Key Attributes and Benefits

Capital Efficiency: Long-term options require a fraction of the capital needed to purchase the underlying asset outright, offering leverage that can amplify returns.

Time Decay Mitigation: By choosing options with longer expirations, traders can reduce the impact of time decay, preserving the option's value over a more extended period.

Volatility Exposure: Longer-term options are less sensitive to short-term price fluctuations in the underlying asset, providing a steadier position that maintains value.

b. Short-term Options: The Income Component

Conversely, short-term options, puts or calls, are sold at the same strike price and have a shorter expiration date. The primary purpose of selling these options is to generate income through the premiums received, which can offset the cost of the long-term options purchased.

Key Attributes and Benefits

Income Generation: The premiums collected from selling short-term put options provide near term income, which can be used to offset the cost of the long-term calls, reduce the overall risk of the position, or be reinvested.

Time Decay Advantage: Short-term options are more heavily affected by time decay, working in the trader's favor as the seller of these options. As time passes, the value of these options diminishes, potentially leading to profitable buy-back opportunities at a lower price.

Flexibility for Adjustments: The short-term nature of these options allows traders to adjust their positions more frequently, responding to market changes or reevaluating strategies without a long-term commitment.

D. Synergy between Long-term and Short-term Options

The interconnection between long-term and short-term options in Batman and Calendar Spreads is what makes this strategy particularly potent. The longer-term option minimizes time decay, while the short-term option generates income and provides opportunities for tactical adjustments based on small market movements. The best way to evaluate the relationship between these position legs is to analyze a Profit and Loss Graph. This is the P&L Graph for a position that we will evaluate later in the book.

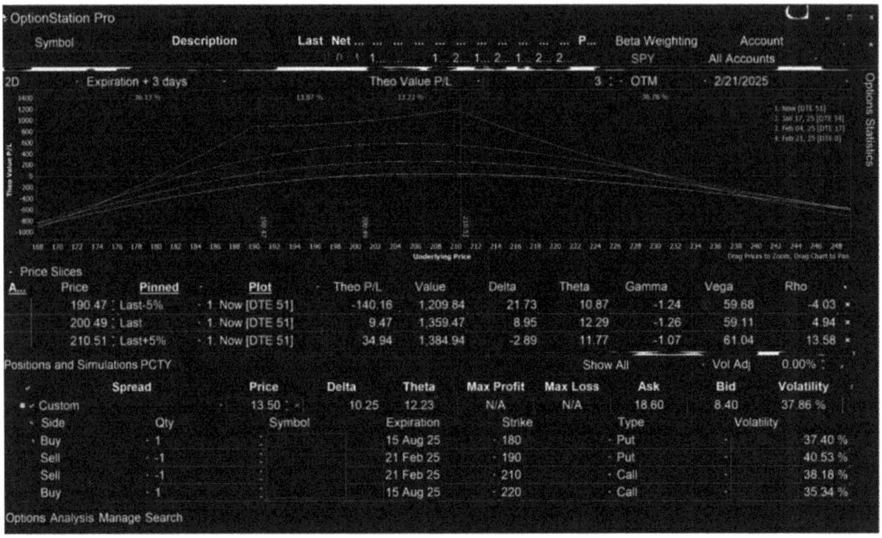

Note: Description of the Profit and Loss Chart with Option Greeks: This chart illustrates the theoretical profit and loss (P&L) of various option positions relative to changes in the underlying asset's price. The x-axis represents the price of the underlying asset, while the y-axis shows the theoretical P&L in dollar terms. Multiple lines on the chart represent different option positions, each with its own expiration date and strike price.

Option Greeks Impact:

Delta: This Greek measures the rate of change of the option's price with respect to the underlying asset's price. In the chart, the slope of each line represents the delta of the option; steeper slopes indicate higher deltas, meaning the option's price is more sensitive to changes in the underlying price.

Gamma: This represents the rate of change of delta with respect to the underlying price. High gamma would show a more pronounced curvature in the P&L lines, indicating how quickly delta changes as the underlying price moves.

Theta: The decay of the option's value over time, or time decay. Since the chart shows expiration in three days, theta's effect would be significant, reducing the option's value as it approaches expiration, flattening the P&L lines over time.

Vega: Measures sensitivity to volatility. While not directly shown, an increase in Vega would widen the P&L range, showing higher potential gains or losses due to changes in implied volatility.

Rho: Sensitivity to interest rate changes, which might not be as visually represented but affects the option's value subtly.

This chart helps traders visualize how their option positions will perform under various market conditions, considering the Greeks' impact on option pricing dynamics.

Strategic Balance: This combination allows traders to balance their exposure to market movements, leveraging the potential for long-term gains while mitigating risks and generating income in the short term.

Adjustment Opportunities: As market conditions change, traders have the flexibility to roll out short-term options, either extending their expiration, adjusting strike prices, or both to adapt the strategy to the current market outlook and objectives.

E. Setting the stage for advanced campaign trading approaches

In the evolving landscape of options trading, the ability to adapt and refine strategies in response to market conditions is paramount. This section aims to bridge the foundational aspects of Batman and Calendar Spreads with practical examples and complete explanation of the factors needed to make trading decisions.

1. Embracing Complexity with Strategy

Advanced campaign trading transcends the basics of buying and selling individual options contracts. It involves a series of coordinated moves, akin to a campaign, where each decision is part of a larger strategy designed to navigate through various market conditions towards achieving specific financial goals.

Strategic Foundation: Batman and Calendar Spreads lay the groundwork by teaching the importance of leveraging time decay, volatility, and possibly a small directional bias in a controlled manner.

Building Complexity: From this foundation, traders can explore more complex arrangements, such as integrating additional legs into the spread to further control risk or enhance returns.

2. Dynamic Adjustments and Decision Making

A hallmark of advanced campaign trading is the dynamic nature of strategy adjustments. Unlike static strategies, campaign trading requires ongoing analysis and adjustments to optimize performance and manage risk. Each market movement or change in the underlying stock's behavior may necessitate a reassessment of the current position and potential adjustments.

- **Developing Alternatives**: Traders must be adept at identifying multiple adjustment paths, each tailored to different market developments.

- **Decision Trees**: Visual tools that map out potential decisions and their outcomes, helping traders to anticipate and plan for multiple market scenarios.
- **Risk and Reward Analysis**: Visual representations of data that can highlight the varying degrees of risk and potential return across different strike prices and expirations.
- **Ranking of Alternative Adjustments**: Not all adjustments are created equal. The use of analytical tools and methods to rank adjustments ensures that traders can make informed decisions that align with their risk tolerance and strategic objectives.
- **Technical Analysis**: Once we have established the use of the previously described tools, we will present best approaches to integrating Technical Analysis into decision process.

Conclusion

Batman and Calendar Spreads are a foundational strategy to Campaign Trading, especially for markets that are expected to remain range bound. By mastering the art of making dynamic adjustments and employing sophisticated analytical tools, traders can position themselves to capitalize on market opportunities with greater confidence and strategic insight. As we move forward, we will delve deeper into these concepts, equipping you with the knowledge and skills needed to thrive in the complex world of options trading.

2

Initial Position Setup and Considerations

A. Criteria for selecting the underlying stock: volatility, trend, and liquidity

The cornerstone of successful Batman and Calendar Spreads lies in the careful selection of the underlying stock. This decision is not merely about choosing a stock that is expected to remain fairly stable without making big directional moves, but it also involves a nuanced evaluation of the stock's volatility and liquidity. These factors play pivotal roles in the strategy's potential success and the ease with which adjustments can be made. This section delves into each criterion, providing a roadmap for selecting an optimal underlying stock for your Batman and Calendar Spreads.

1. Volatility: The Double-Edged Sword

Volatility measures the degree of variation in a stock's price over time. For Batman and Calendar Spreads, an ideal underlying stock exhibits moderate to high volatility. This level of volatility enhances the potential for profit, as the strategy thrives on fat premiums built into the short puts. But this is a little tricky since we also want a stock that is not expected to make big directional moves, at least in our trading timeframe.

Moderate Volatility: This offers a balance between risk and potential return, providing enough price movement to benefit the spread without excessive risk.

High Volatility: Can lead to higher premiums on the options, especially for the short-term leg, increasing the income component of the spread. However, it also comes with greater risk, requiring more diligent monitoring and readiness to adjust.

Note: Finding stocks that have been trading with higher volatility than is expected going forward for an underlying stock is ideal. Finding these better stocks to build Batman and Calendar Spreads around is discussed in Chapter 9.

2. Trend: Neutral Directional Bias

The underlying stock's trend is crucial in aligning the Batman and Calendar Spreads with the anticipated market direction. Since this strategy profits from a neutral move in the stock's price. The perfect candidate is a stock that has been volatile, and this has increased the options Implied Volatility but now the stock is expected to remain fairly neutral in a fairly tight trading range. For those professional investors (a high percentage) who preach that making timing predictions is impossible this would seem foolish.

Often, my preference is to identify stocks that have dropped in price due to an announcement in a market that is trending upwards or to choose a stock that has experienced an upward move due to an announcement in a negative or uncertain market environment. These counter-trends can cause stocks to remain in a fairly tight price range for a period of time.

Note: Of course, if we are truthful the optimum money is made on these trades if the stock is trading close to the initial underlying stock price. If the stock moves a lot but ends up close to the short puts strike price at our short put expiration date the trade is still a good one.

3. Liquidity: The Facilitator of Flexibility

Liquidity in the context of options trading refers to the ease with which options can be bought and sold without causing significant price movements. High liquidity is essential for the components of Batman and Calendar Spreads, ensuring tighter bid-ask spreads and the ability to enter and exit positions efficiently.

Volume and Open Interest: High trading volume and open interest in the options market indicate strong liquidity, reducing the cost of trades and facilitating smoother adjustments. You don't want to open positions with very illiquid options and then pay a lot to make needed adjustments. This will eat into your profits.

Impact on Adjustments: Underlying liquidity allows for quicker responses to market changes, a critical aspect of managing Batman and Calendar Spreads, especially when adjustments are needed to counteract unfavorable market movements.

Note: Liquidity can be built into search criteria and used to filter out stocks that may not support our best stock choice ideal. See Chapter 9.

4. Practical Application

When selecting an underlying stock for a Batman or Calendar Diagonal Spread, traders should perform a comprehensive analysis, considering the stock's volatility, trend, and liquidity. This process involves:

Volatility Analysis: Utilizing historical volatility data and forecasting tools to gauge expected price movements. Batman or Calendar Spreads with short ATM options can experience a drop in volatility, so analysis of the historical volatility trend is important. I like to open these spreads with higher recent volatility.

Trend Evaluation: Employ technical analysis to identify stocks in a stable environment, confirming the neutral directional bias necessary for the strategy.

Liquidity Check: Examining the options market for the stock, focusing on volume, open interest, and bid-ask spreads to ensure sufficient liquidity.

B. Choosing the right long and short options: strike price and expiration dates

Once the underlying stock for a Batman or Calendar Spread is selected, the next critical steps are choosing the appropriate strike prices and expiration dates for both the long and short options. These decisions are instrumental in shaping the risk/reward profile of the strategy, influencing its profitability and manageability. This section provides guidance on selecting these parameters to optimize the setup of your positions.

1. **Batman Spreads**

a. **Selecting the Strike Price**

The strike price determines at what price level the option can be exercised. For a Batman Spread, the choice of strike prices for both the long and short options is a balancing act between maximizing potential profit and managing risk.

Long Option (Buy): The strike prices of the long options (both puts and calls) should be significantly out-of-the-money (OTM) relative to the current price of the underlying stock on the up and down-side. If the stock is trading at 193, choose a 200 to 215 strike price for your long call and a 185 to 175 strike price for your long put.

Short Option (Sell): The strike price for the short option (both puts and calls) is typically close to the being at-the-money (ATM) or slightly OTM, on both sides of the price of the underlying stock. This choice aims to maximize the premium received while keeping a reasonable buffer against the underlying stock's price movements. For the above example, for a stock trading at 193, choose a 195 to 200 strike price for your short call and a 190 to 185 strike price for your short put.

b. **Choosing Expiration Dates**

The expiration dates for the long and short options significantly affect the strategy's performance, particularly in terms of time decay and the trade's overall duration.

Long Option (Buy): Selecting a longer-term expiration date for the long options allows the strategy to weather short-term volatility while buffering against any upward or downward movement of the underlying stock. This choice mitigates the negative impact of time decay on the long position. I typically select long puts or calls that are 5 or 6 months in the future.

Short Option (Sell): The short options, both puts or calls, should have a shorter-term expiration date. This capitalizes on the rapid acceleration of time decay close to expiration, enhancing the income component of the strategy through the decay of the short options' premiums. I typically select short puts or calls that are 30 to 45 days from expiration.

c. Balancing Strike Prices and Expirations

The interplay between the strike prices and expiration dates is where the art of crafting a Batman Spread truly lies. The goal is to establish a position that benefits from the underlying stock's expected neutral to mildly directional movement, collects premiums from the short options, and manages risk effectively. It is possible to find Batman Spreads where the long and short puts are at close to the same price or even offer a Credit Spread for the opening position. This is best seen by using a Profit and Loss Graph.

By carefully selecting the right long and short options, traders can create Batman Spreads that leverage the strengths of this strategy while navigating the complexities of the options market. Through strategic choices and dynamic adjustments, traders can enhance their potential for profit and manage risk in a controlled, thoughtful manner.

2. Calendar Spreads

a. Selecting the Strike Price

The strike price determines at what price level the option can be exercised. For Calendar Spreads, the choice of strike price for both the long and short options is a balancing act between maximizing potential profit and managing risk.

Long Option (Buy): The strike price of the long option should be close to at-the-money (ATM) relative to the current price of the underlying stock.

Short Option (Sell): The strike price of the short option should also be close to at-the-money (ATM) relative to the current price of the underlying stock and the same as the long option strike price. This choice aims to maximize the premium received while keeping a reasonable buffer against the underlying stock's price movements.

b. Choosing Expiration Dates

The expiration dates for the long and short options significantly affect the strategy's performance, particularly in terms of time decay and the trade's overall duration.

Long Option (Buy): Selecting a longer-term expiration date for the long option allows the strategy to weather short-term volatility while buffering against the anticipated upward trend in the underlying stock. This choice mitigates the negative impact of time decay on the long position. I typically select a long put that is 5 or 6 months in the future.

Short Option (Sell): The short option should have a shorter-term expiration date. This capitalizes on the rapid acceleration of time decay close to expiration, enhancing the income component of the strategy through the decay of the short option's premium. I typically select a short put that is 30 to 45 days from expiration.

c. Balancing Strike Prices and Expirations

The interplay between the strike prices and expiration dates is where the art of crafting a Calendar Spread truly lies. The goal is to establish a position that benefits from the underlying stock's expected fairly tight trading range, collects premiums from the short options, and manages risk effectively. It is possible to find Calendar Spread Skews where the long and short puts are at close to the same price for the opening position.

By carefully selecting the right long and short options, traders can create Calendar Spreads that leverage the strengths of this strategy while navigating the complexities of the options market. Through strategic choices and dynamic adjustments, traders can enhance their potential for profit and manage risk in a controlled, thoughtful manner.

C. Initial risk assessment and potential rewards

The allure of Batman and Calendar Spreads lies not only in their strategic complexity but in their ability to balance risk with potential rewards. A thorough initial risk assessment and a clear understanding of the possible rewards are critical components of any successful trading strategy. This section delves into evaluating these aspects for these spreads, providing traders with a framework for making informed decisions from the onset of their trading campaign.

1. Assessing Risk

Risk assessment in Batman and Calendar Spreads involves understanding the maximum potential loss, the impact of time decay, and the volatility of the underlying stock. Here's how traders can navigate these factors:

- **Maximum Potential Loss**: The initial buying power (and potential loss) required to establish these neutral spreads is significantly different:

Batman Spreads: If a Batman is established with both puts and calls using puts for the below the underlying stock price position (essentially a put based bullish diagonal spread) then the buying power for this half of the position is the same as required for a bullish diagonal spread using puts. The upper half of the position using calls is the same as if calls are used to establish a bearish diagonal spread using calls. With both diagonals in place a Batman Spread is opened.

Calendar Spreads: A Calendar Spread can also be established using puts or calls. In both cases the buying power required is simply the price of the long option (put or call) minus the price of the short option. This will be a debit spread.

Note: Profits are higher, and risk will be easier to manage if positions are built around a stock where the Implied Volatility of the short leg is higher than the Implied Volatility of the short leg. See Chapter 9.

❖ **Time Decay (Theta):** Time decay impacts the long and short positions differently. While the short option's time decay can benefit the trader by eroding its value over time, the long option's value also decreases as expiration approaches. Balancing these effects is key to managing the spread's overall risk.

❖ **Volatility Impact:** An unexpected decrease in implied volatility can diminish the value of both options but will typically have a greater impact on the short put because it is closer to the initial strike price. An increase in volatility could enhance the position's value in a shorter timeframe.

2. Evaluating Potential Rewards

The potential rewards of a Batman or Calendar Spread are primarily driven by the income generated from the decay of the short option's premium.

Optimal Outcome: The ideal scenario occurs when the underlying stock remains close to the strike price of the short option (s) at expiration. This maintains the value of the long option while allowing the short options to expire worthless, capturing the full premium as profit.

Income Generation: The systematic selling of short-term options against a longer-term long position creates an opportunity for regular income. This income can offset the cost of the long option or be reinvested to adjust the position.

3. Balancing Risk and Reward

The key to mastering Batman and Calendar Spreads lies in the trader's ability to balance the inherent risks with the potential rewards. This balance involves strategic selection of strike prices and expiration dates, as well as ongoing adjustments based on market conditions.

Strategic Adjustments: Traders must be prepared to make adjustments to the spread in response to market movements or changes in the underlying stock's volatility. These adjustments can include rolling the short option to a different strike or expiration or even adjusting the long position if necessary.

Use of Analytical Tools: Decision trees, risk analysis, and choice optimization can provide valuable insights into the probability of various outcomes, helping traders to make informed decisions about adjustments and manage their risk/reward balance more effectively.

D. Practical examples of opening Batman Spreads

Batman Spreads offer traders a consistent way to capitalize on expected neutral to mildly directional movements in the underlying stock while managing risk and generating income. To illustrate the application of this strategy, let's use practical examples that demonstrate how to establish Batman Spreads, taking into account the selection of the underlying stock, strike prices, expiration dates, risk assessment, and potential rewards.

1. Example 1: Neutral Expectation for an HR/Payroll Software Company

Scenario: A trader anticipates that an established HR/Payroll software platform stock will remain in a tight trading range over the next month and possibly drift upward with the market.

Underlying Stock: ABC, currently trading at $200.

Long Option: Buys 2 ea. 7-month out put options with a strike price of $180 (OTM) for a premium of $12.00 and

Buys 2 ea. 7-month out call options with a strike price of $220 (OTM) for a premium of $16.20.

Short Option: Sells 2 ea. 6-weeks out put options with a strike price of $190 (OTM) for a premium of $7.20 and

Sells 2 ea. 6-weeks out call options with a strike price of $210 (OTM) for a premium of $7.10.

Rationale: The long put is chosen OTM to benefit from less time decay, and the short put is ATM to generate income.

Profit and Loss Graph for this Position

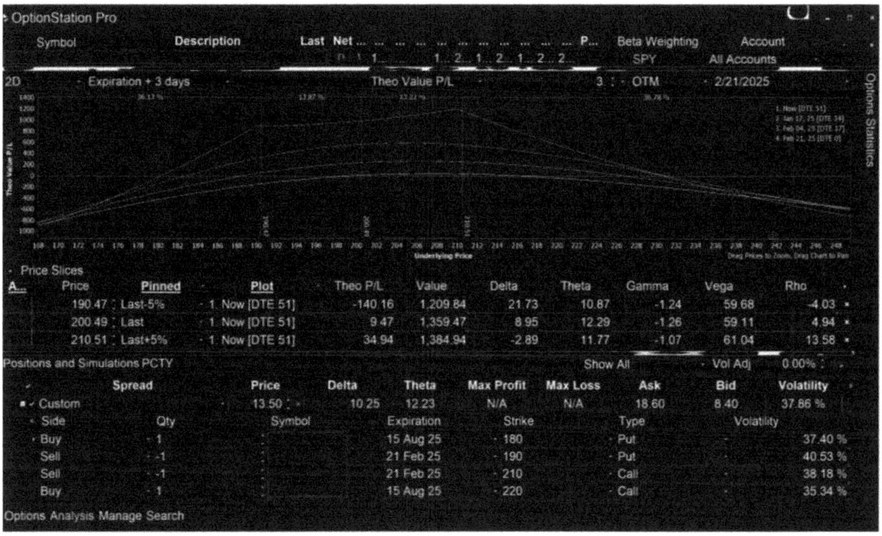

Risk Assessment: The net debit (and maximum potential loss) for the **put diagonal** is \$4.8 (\$12 - \$7.20) + \$10 (difference in strike prices) = \$14.80 x 1 x 100 = \$1480 as shown below.

The net debit (and maximum potential loss) for the call diagonal is \$9.1 (\$16.20 - \$7.10) + \$10 (difference in strike prices) = 19.10 x 1 x 100 = \$1910 as shown below.

The risk is the stock moving down significantly from the opening price or moving up too rapidly. This yields a **total potential loss** of this position of **\$1480 + \$1910 = \$3390.**

Potential Rewards: The ideal outcome is for ABC to close very close to \$210 as the short put and call expires, allowing the trader to keep the short premium while the long put maintains its price due to slower decay.

Example 1 Position Greeks and Information

Position	# of Options and Price	Buying Power (BP) Needed	Why Making Investment or Adjustment
Initial Batman Spread			
Long ABC August 15th 180 Put	1 @ 12.00	[($14.80 x 100 = $1480)] + [($19.10 x 100 = $1910)] = Total = $3390	Long options have slower decay than the short options, indicated by the lower Theta. Significant profit from decay in 1 month. The Theta will increase as options approach expiration.
Short ABC February 21st 190 Put	1 @ 7.20		
Long ABC August 15th 220 Call	1 @ 16.20		
Short ABC February 21st 210 Call	1 @ 7.10		

2. Example 2: Anticipating steady growth in a Diversified Industrial Products Solution Company

Scenario: A diversified industrials products solution company is expected to see a gradual uptick in its stock price over the next year due to steady but slow earnings growth.

Underlying Stock: DEF, currently trading at $129.

Long Option: Buys 2 ea. 6-month out put options with a strike price of $115 (OTM) for a premium of $5.10 and

Buys 2 ea. 6-month out call options with a strike price of $145 (OTM) for a premium of $5.45.

Short Option: Sells 2 ea. 5-weeks out put options with a strike price of $123 (OTM) for a premium of $2.50 and

Sells 2 ea. 5-weeks out call options with a strike price of $135 (OTM) for a premium of $3.25.

Rationale: The long-term OTM put is selected for its delta and lower theta, ensuring the position benefits from upward movement with reduced time decay. The short-term OTM call is chosen for income generation and to benefit from rapid time decay.

Profit and Loss Graph for this Position

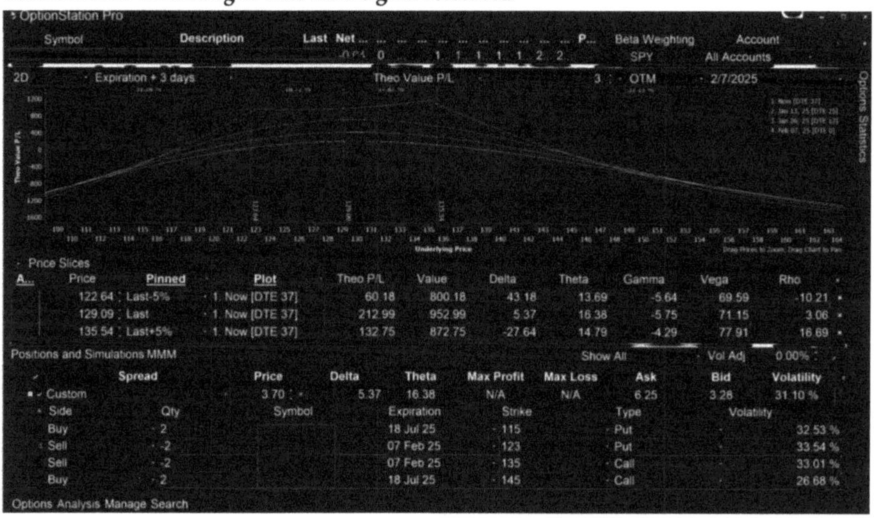

Note: This chart helps traders visualize how their option positions will perform under various market conditions, considering the Greeks' impact on option pricing dynamics.

Risk Assessment: The net debit (and maximum potential loss) for the **put diagonal** is $2.6 ($5.10 - $2.50) + $8 (difference in strike prices) = $10.60 x 2 x 100 = $2120 as shown below.

The net debit (and maximum potential loss) for the call diagonal is $2.2 ($5.45 - $3.25) + $10 (difference in strike prices) = 12.20 x 2 x 100 = $2440 as shown below.

The risk is the stock moving down significantly from the opening price or moving up too rapidly. This yields a **total potential loss** of this position of **$2120 + $2440 = $4560.**

Potential Rewards: The ideal outcome is for DEF to close very close to $135 as the short puts and calls expire, allowing the trader to keep the short premium while the long put maintains its price due to slower decay.

Example 2 Position Greeks and Information

Position	# of Options and Price	Buying Power (BP) Needed	Why Making Investment or Adjustment
Initial Batman Spread			
Long DEF July 18th 115 Put	2 @ 5.10	[($21.20 x 100 = $2120)] + [($24.40 x 100 = $2440)] = Total = $4560	Slower decay for the long options, indicated by the lower Theta. Significant profit from decay in 1 month. The Theta will increase as options approach expiration.
Short DEF February 7th 123 Put	2 @ 2.50		
Long DEF July 18th 145 Call	2 @ 5.45		
Short DEF February 7th 135 Call	2 @ 3.25		

3. Thinking Ahead to Possible Adjustments based on Changes in Underlying Stock Prices

Each example outlines a situation where market conditions could necessitate adjustments:

Rolling the Short Option: If the underlying stock moves so that either of the short options are In-the-money at expiration, the trader might roll it to a higher strike and/or a later expiration to capture more premium and avoid assignment. Or there are several other possible adjustments that can be made.

Managing the Long Option: If the stock rises sharply, making the long calls worth more, the trader could sell it for a profit and possibly set up a new spread with adjusted expectations or close the position for a profit.

E. Practical examples of opening Calendar Spreads

Calendar Spreads offer traders a simple way to capitalize on an expected tight trading range in the underlying stock while managing risk and generating income. To illustrate the application of this strategy, let's dive into practical examples that demonstrate how to establish Calendar Spreads, taking into account the selection of the underlying stock, strike prices, expiration dates, risk assessment, and potential rewards.

1. Example 1: Neutral to Drift Up Expectation in a Credit Trading Platform

Scenario: A trader anticipates that an established credit trading platform stock will remain in a tight trading range over the next 2 months and possibly drift upward with the market.

Underlying Stock: XYZ, currently trading at $226.

Long Option: Buys 2 ea. 7-month output options with a strike price of $230 (ATM) for a premium of $21.30.

Short Option: Sells 2 ea. 6-weeks output options with a strike price of $230 (ATM) for a premium of $12.30.

Rationale: The long options will benefit from less time decay, and the short options are ATM to generate income.

Profit and Loss Graph for this Position

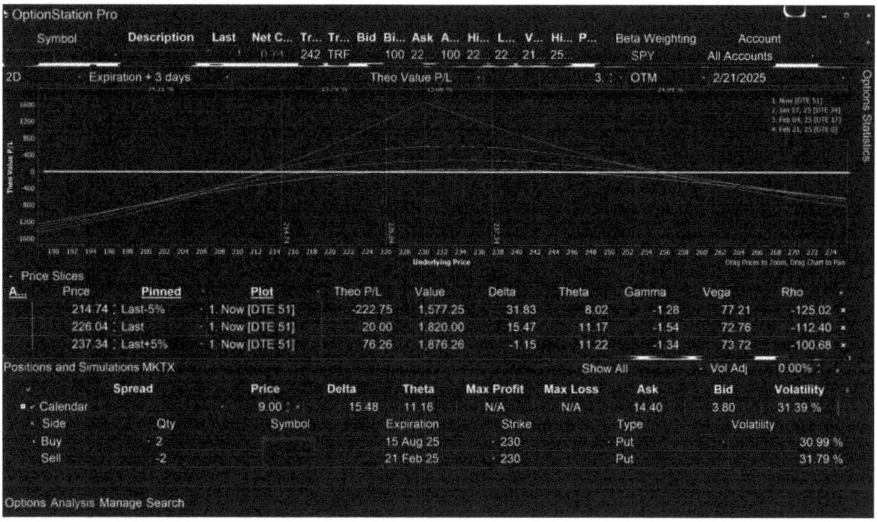

Note: This chart helps traders visualize how their option positions will perform under various market conditions, considering the Greeks' impact on option pricing dynamics.

Risk Assessment: The net debit (and maximum potential loss) is 2 x \$9.00 (\$21.30 - \$12.30) = 18 x 100 as shown below. The risk is the stock moving down significantly from the opening price or moving up too rapidly. This yields a **total potential loss** of this position of **\$1800.**

Potential Rewards: The ideal outcome is for XYZ to close very close to \$230 as the short call expires, allowing the trader to keep the short premium while the long put maintains its price due to slower decay.

Example 1 Position Greeks and Information

Position	# of Options and Price	Buying Power (BP) Needed	Why Making Investment or Adjustment
Initial Calendar Spread			
Long XYZ August 15th 230 Put	2 @ 21.30	$9 x 100 = $900 x 2 = $1800	Slower decay than the short put, indicated by the lower Theta. Significant profit from decay in 1 month. The Theta will increase as options approach expiration.
Short XYZ February 21st 230 Put	2 @ 12.30		

2. Example 2: Anticipating steady growth in a Semiconductor Solution Company

Scenario: A semiconductor solution is expected to see steady but not exciting growth over the next quarter.

Underlying Stock: UVW, currently trading at $132.

Long Option: Buys 3 ea. 5-month out put options with a strike price of $135 (ATM) for a premium of $29.10.

Short Option: Sells 3 ea. 7-weeks out put options with a strike price of $135 (ATM) for a premium of $17.00.

Rationale: The long-term ATM put is selected for its delta and lower theta, ensuring the position benefits from a neutral movement with reduced time decay. The short-term ATM call is chosen for income generation and to benefit from rapid time decay.

Profit and Loss Graph for this Position

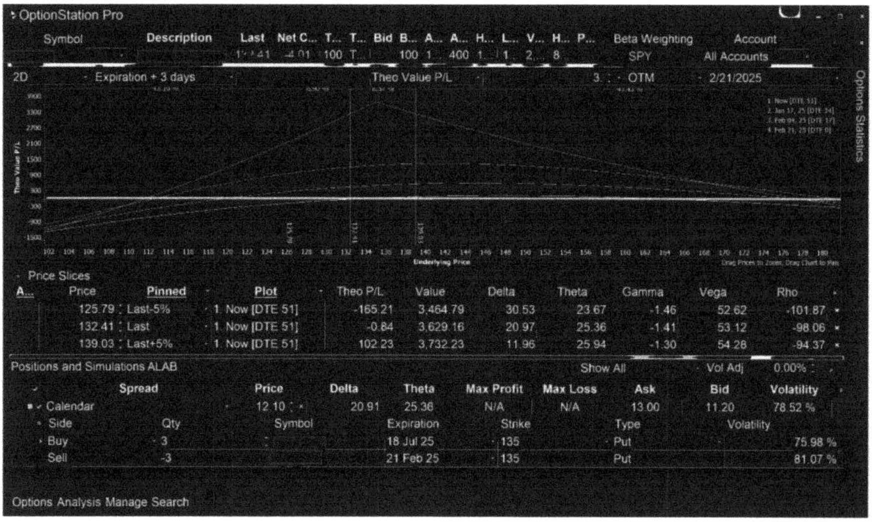

Note: This chart helps traders visualize how their option positions will perform under various market conditions, considering the Greeks' impact on option pricing dynamics.

Risk Assessment: The net debit for each calendar spread is $12.10 ($29.10 - $17.00) and the total buy power required for this spread is 3 x $1210 ($12.10 x 100), representing the maximum potential loss of $3630, as shown below if UVW drops significantly. This yields a **total potential loss** of this position of **$3630.**

Potential Rewards: The ideal outcome is for UVW to close very close to $135 as the short call expires, allowing the trader to keep the short premium while the long put maintains its price due to slower decay.

Example 2 Position Greeks and Information

Position	# of Options and Price	Buying Power (BP) Needed	Why Making Investment or Adjustment
Initial Calendar Spread			
Long UVW July 18th 135 Put	3 @ 29.10	$12.10 x 100 = $1210 x 3 = $3630	Slower decay than the short put, indicated by the lower Theta.
Short UVW February 21st 135 Put	3 @ 17.00		Significant profit from decay in 1 month. The Theta will increase as options approach expiration.

3. Thinking Ahead to Possible Adjustments based on Changes in Underlying Stock Prices

Each example outlines a situation where market conditions could necessitate adjustments:

Rolling the Short Option: If the underlying stock exceeds the short put's strike price at expiration, the trader might roll it to a higher strike and/or a later expiration to capture more premium and avoid assignment.

Managing the Long Option: If the falls sharply, making the long put Deep In The Money (DITM), the trader could sell it for a profit and possibly set up a new spread with adjusted expectations or close the position for a profit.

Conclusion

These practical examples underscore the importance of selecting appropriate options, conducting a thorough risk assessment, and being prepared to make strategic adjustments. Through these steps, traders can harness the power of Batman and Calendar Spreads to achieve a balanced approach to options trading, capitalizing on expected market movements while managing risk effectively.

3

Market Conditions and Adjustment Decisions

A. Monitoring market conditions: key indicators and signals

In the dynamic world of options trading, continuously monitoring market conditions is crucial for managing Batman and Calendar Spreads effectively. This ability not only aids in the initial positioning but is also pivotal for making timely adjustments as market conditions evolve. This section focuses on the key indicators and signals traders should monitor to navigate the complexities of the market, ensuring their Batman and Calendar Spreads are optimally positioned for success.

1. Economic Indicators

Economic indicators are vital tools for gauging the overall health of the economy and predicting future market movements. Key indicators include:

Gross Domestic Product (GDP): Reflects the economy's total output and growth rate, influencing market sentiment and stock prices.

Unemployment Rate: High unemployment rates can signal economic distress, potentially affecting consumer spending and signaling weaker corporate earnings ahead.

Consumer Price Index (CPI): An inflation measure that impacts consumer purchasing power, monetary policy, and, consequently, stock market trends.

Interest Rates: Set by central banks, interest rates affect borrowing costs for consumers and corporations, influencing equity valuations and market direction.

The Purchasing Managers' Index (PMI): An economic indicator derived from monthly surveys of private sector companies. It measures the prevailing direction of economic trends in service and manufacturing sectors, indicating expansion when above 50 and contraction when below.

2. Technical Analysis Indicators

Technical analysis provides insight into market psychology and potential future movements of stock prices through the study of past market data, primarily price and volume. Essential technical indicators include:

Moving Averages: Indicates the average stock price over a specific period, helping identify trends. The crossing of short-term and long-term moving averages can signal shifts in market direction.

Relative Strength Index (RSI): Measures the speed and change of price movements, indicating overbought or oversold conditions that may precede a market reversal.

Bollinger Bands: Consist of a moving average between two standard deviation lines, indicating volatility. A stock breaking through the bands may signal a continuation or reversal.

Volume: High trading volume can confirm trends or signal reversals when accompanied by significant price changes.

3. Market Sentiment Indicators

Understanding market sentiment can provide clues about the market's future direction, aiding in the timing of adjustments for Batman and Calendar Spreads.

Volatility Index (VIX): Often referred to as the "fear index," the VIX measures market risk and investors' sentiments towards future market conditions.

Put/Call Ratio: The ratio of put options traded to call options traded. A high ratio suggests bearish sentiment, while a low ratio indicates bullish sentiment.

Advancers/Decliners Ratio: This ratio between the number of stocks that closed higher versus those that closed lower provides insight into the market's breadth and sentiment.

4. Monitoring and Adjustment Strategies

Effective monitoring of these indicators necessitates a disciplined approach, incorporating regular reviews of economic data, technical analysis, and sentiment indicators. This comprehensive surveillance enables traders to anticipate market movements and adjust their Batman and Calendar Spreads accordingly.

Economic Trends: Adjust positions in anticipation of economic downturns or upswings based on GDP, unemployment rates, CPI, and interest rates.

Technical Breakouts or Reversals: Use technical indicators to identify potential entry or exit points for adjustments, especially when trends confirm or refute your market outlook.

Sentiment Shifts: Respond to changes in market sentiment as indicated by the VIX, put/call ratios, and advancers/decliners ratios, adjusting spread positions to align with the prevailing market mood.

B. Developing a systematic approach to adjustments

For Batman and Calendar Spreads, a systematic approach to making adjustments is not just beneficial, it's crucial for success. This section lays the foundation for a disciplined, methodical approach to adjusting positions in response to market dynamics to maximize profits and minimize losses.

1. Understanding the Need for a System

Adjustments to Batman and Calendar Spreads are not mere reactions to market movements but are strategic decisions that require careful consideration. A systematic approach ensures that these adjustments are made consistently, logically, and in alignment with the trader's overarching goals and risk management strategy.

2. Components of a Systematic Adjustment Approach

Criteria for Making Adjustments:

Price Triggers: Identify specific price levels of the underlying stock that necessitate adjustments. These can be based on technical analysis, such as support and resistance levels or key moving averages.

Volatility Changes: Changes in implied volatility can significantly impact option prices. Set volatility thresholds that trigger an evaluation of potential adjustments.

Time Decay (Theta): As expiration approaches, the impact of time decay on both the long and short options must be monitored. Establish time-based criteria for considering adjustments.

Economic and Geopolitical Events: Plan for adjustments around key events that can cause market volatility, ensuring positions are optimally configured to manage risk.

Rules for Entering Opening Trades: Don't chase an opening position. Always set the price that you will accept above or below what the market is offering and let the stock and related option prices meet your limit orders. Sometimes it is best to set limits pretty far beyond what the market is offering and then improve your limit in a measured manner until you are filled.

By adeptly navigating earnings reports, economic announcements, and geopolitical events, traders can better manage the inherent risks and opportunities within their Batman and Calendar Spreads. Proactive and reactive adjustments, guided by thorough analysis and a keen understanding of market sentiment, are essential for maintaining the resilience and profitability of these positions in a constantly evolving market landscape.

C. Adjusting the long and short positions: timing and techniques

The ability to adjust the components of Batman and Calendar Spreads—both the long and short positions—is crucial for managing the strategy effectively in response to changing market conditions. This section explores the timing and techniques for adjusting these positions, enhancing the strategy's flexibility and potential for profit while managing risk.

1. Timing Adjustments

Key Signals for Adjustment:

Significant Movements in the Underlying Stock: A sharp rise or fall in the stock price may necessitate adjustments to maintain the desired risk/reward profile.

Changes in Volatility: An increase or decrease in implied volatility can impact the value of both the long and short options, prompting a reassessment.

Approaching Expiration of the Short Option: As the short option nears expiration, especially if it is in or near the money, traders need to decide whether to roll the option to a new position or let it expire and adjust the strategy accordingly.

Economic, Earnings, and Geopolitical Events: Anticipated or unexpected events may require preemptive adjustments to hedge against volatility or capitalize on predicted movements.

2. Techniques for Adjusting Long Positions

Rolling Up or Out:

If the underlying stock has risen significantly, a long option might be far OTM but still hold value. Rolling up (to a higher strike) or out (to a later expiration) may be necessary to reach profitability when the short put expires. As we will see when discussing adjustments there are numerous possible moves that can be made.

Adjusting for Defense: In a market downturn, consider rolling the long option down (to a lower strike) to decrease the position's delta, making it less sensitive to further declines.

3. Techniques for Adjusting Short Positions

Rolling Short Puts:

Rolling Up: If the stock's price approaches the short options' strike, rolling to the same or different strike price may be necessary to give the position more time to reach profitability.

Rolling Out: Extending the expiration of the short put allows for continued premium collection and can be used to manage short-term moves against the position.

Closing the Short Put: In some cases, it may be advantageous to let the short option expire and then consider what to do about the long leg.

Combining Adjustments: In practice, adjustments to the long and short positions may be combined to optimize the Batman and Calendar Spreads based on current market analysis and future expectations. For example, rolling the short put down and out while simultaneously rolling the long put to a lower strike can adjust for a more extreme outlook than initially anticipated.

Conclusion

Adjusting the long and short positions within Batman and Calendar Spreads requires a nuanced understanding of market signals, the flexibility to respond to changes, and the strategic use of various techniques to optimize the position. By mastering the timing and techniques of adjustments, and employing a combination of keen market observation, understanding of adjustment techniques, and analytical tools, traders can navigate the complexities of the market, making informed decisions to protect their positions and maximize potential returns.

4

Advanced Adjustment Strategies: Batman Spread Example 1

For the first Batman example shown in Chapter 2 we will provide a complete analysis using our tools and show the outcomes in this chapter.

A. Possible Adjustments for Example 1

There are numerous possible adjustments for this initial opening position based on market conditions but for our purposes we will evaluate these:

- Adjustment 1: Sell Long Put and Hold the Short Put and the Long and Short Calls
- Adjustment 2: Hold the Long Puts and Calls and Roll both Short Options
- Adjustment 3: Hold Puts and Long Call and Buy Back Short Call

or

- Close the Position Early (prior to or at expiration of the short options)

B. Decision-Making Framework:

Decision Trees: Utilize decision trees to map out possible adjustment paths and their potential outcomes, providing a clear visual framework for decision-making.

Risk/Reward Analysis: Every potential adjustment should be evaluated in terms of its impact on the risk/reward profile of the position. This involves a thorough analysis of how adjustments might shift the risk exposure and potential returns.

Ranking Based on Probability of Success: Use historical data and analysis tools to rank potential adjustments by their likelihood of success, focusing on those with the highest probability of achieving the desired outcome. Before we do our analysis let's see what ChatGPT can offer.

Prompt

As an expert options trader please describe the best market environment and anticipated movement of the underlying stock for the use of a Batman Spread composed of 1 ea. Long XYZ August 15th 180 Put at a price of 12.00, 1 ea. Short XYZ February 21st 190 Put at a price of 7.20, 1 ea. Long XYZ August 15th 220 Call at a price of 16.20 and 1 ea. Short XYZ February 21st 210 Call at a price of 7.10. Please describe the various stock movements after open and rank the most likely stock movement to yield the trader with a profit. The trade is opened January 2nd when the stock is trading at a price of 200 with volatility of 0.3786.

Response with ChatGPT

A Batman Spread is a neutral-to-directional options strategy designed to take advantage of range-bound movements with the potential to profit from slight directional movement if the underlying stock stays within a defined range for an extended period. The spread, as outlined, involves a combination of long-dated (August 15th) options and short-dated (February 21st) options with both puts and calls, forming a "winged" structure around the current price of $200. Below is an analysis of the best market environment, anticipated movements, and scenarios for profitability.

Best Market Environment for a Batman Spread

Moderate Volatility: The initial implied volatility (IV) of 0.3786 is moderately high, favoring the strategy because the premium collected from the shorter-term options (February) helps offset the cost of the longer-term options (August).

Ideally, volatility should remain stable or slightly decrease. An increase in IV after the short options expire could negatively impact the long options due to increased extrinsic value.

Neutral-to-Slightly-Directional Movement: The Batman Spread performs best in a neutral or slightly directional market where the stock price remains within or near the $190-$210 range until February 21st expiration. Significant movement in either direction may lead to losses if the long options don't offset the decay or the intrinsic value of the short options.

Analysis of Stock Movements

1. Stock Stays Between $190 and $210 Until February 21st (Ideal Case)

Outcome: This is the most profitable scenario.

The February 21st short options (190 Put and 210 Call) expire worthless, allowing the trader to keep the full premium of $7.20 and $7.10, respectively.

After February, the trader holds the August 15th long options, which still retain substantial time value and could benefit from a directional move or increased IV.

Profitability: High.

2. Stock Falls Below $190 Before February 21st

Outcome: Moderately profitable, depending on timing.

The 190 Put (short) incurs a loss as the stock moves lower, but the 180 Put (long) gains value.

After February expiration, the long 180 Put retains value, but profit depends on whether the stock stabilizes or continues lower.

Profitability: Moderate.

3. Stock Rises Above $210 Before February 21st

Outcome: Moderately profitable.

The 210 Call (short) incurs losses as the stock rises, but the 220 Call (long) gains intrinsic value, offsetting the short position.

After February expiration, the long 220 Call remains valuable, especially if the stock continues to rise.

Profitability: Moderate.

4. Stock Moves Outside the $190-$210 Range Immediately After Open

Outcome: Loss is likely.

Early significant movement could cause losses due to the intrinsic value of the February short options increasing before time decay takes effect.

This would also hurt the trader's ability to hold the longer-term August options for further gains.

Profitability: Low.

5. Stock Stays Exactly at $200

Outcome: Highly profitable.

Time decay maximizes the profitability of the February short options.

The long options (August 180 Put and 220 Call) retain their time value without incurring significant losses due to price movement.

Profitability: High.

Ranking the Scenarios for Profitability

Stock remains between $190-$210 until February 21st: Best-case scenario due to maximized time decay of short options and retention of long options' value.

Stock stays at $200: Nearly ideal, with minimal movement leading to maximum theta decay of short options.

Stock rises above $210 (slightly): Gains from the long call offset the losses from the short call.

Stock falls below $190 (slightly): Gains from the long put offset the losses from the short put.

Stock moves significantly outside the range ($190-$210) immediately: Least profitable due to increased intrinsic value of short options early in the trade.

Key Considerations

Time Decay (Theta): This strategy profits heavily from the accelerated time decay of the February options. Patience is crucial to allow this to play out.

Implied Volatility (Vega): Stable or slightly decreasing volatility favors the trade, especially after February expiration.

Directional Risk (Delta): The strategy is relatively neutral but becomes more directional after February options expire.

This Batman Spread strategy is ideal for traders expecting the stock to remain relatively stable within a defined range, with moderate IV and no significant directional shocks in the near term.

The opening position and adjustment characteristics, including the Greeks, are shown for the 4 potential adjustments that we are evaluating.

Position Characteristics at the Adjustment and Outcomes

Position	# of Options and Price	Buying Power (BP) Needed	Why Making Investment or Adjustment
Initial Batman Spread			
Long ABC August 15th 180 Put	1 @ 12.00	[($14.80 x 100 = $1480)] + [($19.10 x 100 = $1910)] = Total = $3390	Long options have slower decay than the short options, indicated by the lower Theta. Significant profit from decay in 1 month. The Theta will increase as options approach expiration.
Short ABC February 21st 190 Put	1 @ 7.20		
Long ABC August 15th 220 Call	1 @ 16.20		

Short ABC February 21st 210 Call	1 @ 7.10		
Adjustment 1: Sell Long Put and Hold the Short Put , the Long and Short Calls : ABC has dropped 20 points from original entry point			
Sell the Long Put	0 @ 31.50	**New BP**: ($19,000 x 0.50) + (($16.20 – $7.10) x 100) + $1000 = $11,410	**Profit**: $((31.50 – 12) x 1 x 100 = $1950 5 months left for stock to recover.
Hold the Short	1 @ 26.80		
Hold Long Call	1 @ 4.30		
Hold Short Call	1 @ 2.2		
Adjustment 2: Hold the Long Puts and Calls and Roll both Short Options: ABC has dropped 10 points from original entry point			
Hold Long Put	1 @ 21.60	**New BP**: [($12 -$6.2) + ($16.2 - 4)] x 100} + $2000 = $3960	Not much premium decay in the long options after 1 month **Profit:** ($7.20 + $7.10) x 100 = $1430
Roll Short Put	1 @ 6.2		
Hold Long Call	1 @ 9.35		
Roll Short Call	1 @ 4		
Adjustment 3: Hold Puts , Long Call and Buy Back Short Call: ABC has risen 10 points from original entry point			
Hold the Long	1 @ 8.45	**New BP**: ($14.80 x 100) – ($19.10 x 100) + ($16.20 x 100) = $1190	**Profit**: $7.1 x 100 = $710
Hold Short Put	1 @ 4		
Hold Long Call	1 @ 24.50		
Buy Back Short Call	0		

	4. Close the Position Early: The short legs are expiring; the Underlying has risen 10 points from the original entry point.		
Sell the Long Put	0	**New BP:** N/A	**Profit:** [($12 - $8.45) + ($7.2 – 0) + ($24.50 – $16.20) + ($7.10 – $0)] x 100 = ($26.15 x 100) = $2615
Buy Back the Short Put	0		
Sell the Long Call	0		
Buy Back the Short Call	0		

Notes:

1) 50% Margin,

2) The Buying Power (BP) Needed column depicts Buying Power for the adjusted position and not the change to the Buying Power.

C. Systematic Response: According to the decision-making framework, the trader evaluates each of the adjustments to determine the best choice for a specific moment.

Decision Tree: Mapped out below for this example.

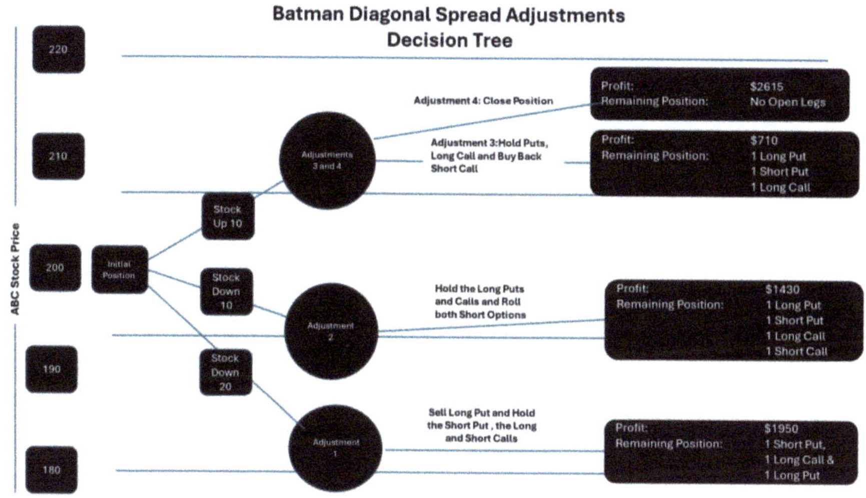

Example 1: Adjustment 1, Sell Long Put and Hold the Short Put and the Long and Short Calls

Scenario: The underlying stock of a Batman Spread experiences a strong bearish move dropping 20 points to 180.

Adjustment: The trader sells the long put leg at a profit and holds the short put leg and the call diagonal.

Position Characteristics At the Adjustment

Position	# of Options and Price	Buying Power (BP) Needed	Why Making Investment or Adjustment
Initial Batman Spread			
Long ABC August 15th 180 Put	1 @ 12.00	[($14.80 x 100 = $1480)] + [($19.10 x 100 = $1910)] = Total = $3390	Long options have slower decay than the short options, indicated by the lower Theta. Significant profit from decay in 1 month. The Theta will increase as options approach expiration.
Short ABC February 21st 190 Put	1 @ 7.20		
Long ABC August 15th 220 Call	1 @ 16.20		
Short ABC February 21st 210 Call	1 @ 7.10		
Adjustment 1: Sell Long Put and Hold the Short Put , the Long and Short Calls : XYZ has dropped 20 points from original entry point			
Sell the Long Put	1 @ 31.50	**New BP**: ($19,000 x 0.50) + (($16.20 – $7.10) x 100) + $1000 = $11,410	**Profit**: $(31.50 – 12) x 1 x 100 = $1950 5 months left for stock to recover.
Hold the Short	1 @ 26.80		
Hold Long Call	1 @ 4.30		
Hold Short Call	1 @ 2.2		

Outcome: The adjustment capitalizes on the increased volatility and in the money increasing delta of the long put leg to extract higher premiums and profits of $1950.

Risk / Reward Analysis: Remaining Risk and Possible Future Adjustments are determined by evaluating the remaining position. The Profit and Loss Graph for the remaining position is below.

Profit and Loss Graph after the Adjustment

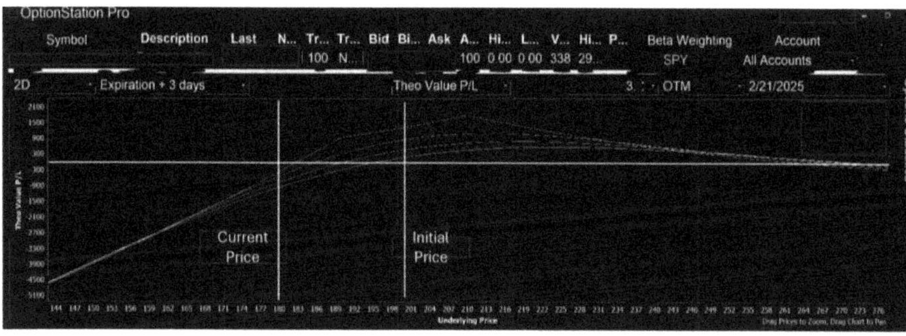

If the stock remains at 180 the new adjusted position will lose a small amount of money. If the stock rises back to the positive profit zone significant more profit can be made. If the stock continues to fall the loss can mount.

What to do Now? Possible Future Adjustments

With profit in hand and a remaining short and long options, the trader will benefit if the underlying stock moves back up. One possible way to manage this situation is to roll the short put at close to the expiration date and also reinstate the short call at the same strike price or lower when the premium is decayed.

Example 1: Adjustment 2, Hold the Long Puts and Calls and Roll both Short Options

Scenario: The underlying stock of a Batman Spread drops 10 points to 190. When the short options expire, the trader can choose to close the position for a profit or roll the short options to a future expiration date. This can continue until the long options expires.

Adjustment: The trader rolls the short options to the same or higher strike, extending the expiration to capture additional premium.

Position Characteristics At the Adjustment

Position	# of Options and Price	Buying Power (BP) Needed	Why Making Investment or Adjustment
Initial Batman Spread			
Long ABC August 15th 180 Put	1 @ 12.00	[($14.80 x 100 = $1480)] + [($19.10 x 100 = $1910)] = Total = $3390	Long options have slower decay than the short options, indicated by the lower Theta. Significant profit from decay in 1 month. The Theta will increase as options approach expiration.
Short ABC February 21st 190 Put	1 @ 7.20		
Long ABC August 15th 220 Call	1 @ 16.20		
Short ABC February 21st 210 Call	1 @ 7.10		
Adjustment 2: Hold the Long Puts and Calls and Roll both Short Options: ABC has dropped 10 points from original entry point			
Hold Long Put	1 @ 21.60	**New BP**: [($12 -$6.2) + ($16.2 -4)] x 100} + $2000 = $3960	Not much decay after 1 month **Profit:** ($7.20 + $7.10) x 100 = $1430
Roll Short Put	1 @ 6.2		
Hold Long Call	1 @ 9.35		
Roll Short Call	1 @ 4		

Outcome: The adjustment capitalizes on the complete decay of the short puts and calls to zero premium but the stock has dropped 10 points to 190, affecting the prices of the long options. Both puts and calls can be rolled to the next month and profits can be taken on both by buying back the shorts when they are rolled. This yields a profit of $1430.

Risk / Reward Analysis: Remaining Risk and Possible Future Adjustments are determined by evaluating the remaining position. The Profit and Loss Graph for the remaining position is below.

Profit and Loss Graph after the Adjustment

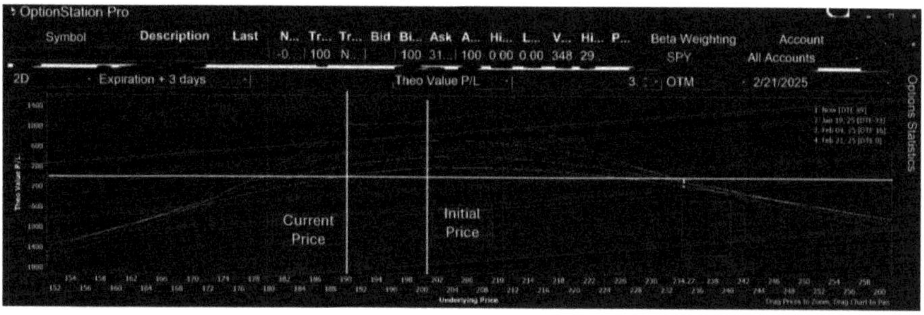

What to do Now? Possible Future Adjustments

With profit in hand from the expired short put, the trader will benefit if the underlying stock stays close to the same price or moves back up some. One possible way to manage this scenario is to hold until the next month when the short options are all decayed away and close the position. That is if the trader is so lucky and the stock does not make more big moves.

Example 1: Adjustment 3, Hold Puts and Long Call and Buy Back Short Call

Scenario: The underlying stock of a Batman Spread experiences a strong bullish rally and the price is now at 210.

Adjustment: The trader buys back the short call and holds the remaining legs.

Position Characteristics At the Adjustment

Position	# of Options and Price	Buying Power (BP) Needed	Why Making Investment or Adjustment
		Initial Batman Spread	
Long ABC August 15th 180 Put	1 @ 12.00	[($14.80 x 100 = $1480)] + [($19.10 x 100 = $1910)] = Total = $3390	Long options have slower decay than the short options, indicated by the lower Theta. Significant profit from decay in 1 month. The Theta will increase as options approach expiration.
Short ABC February 21st 190 Put	1 @ 7.20		
Long ABC August 15th 220 Call	1 @ 16.20		
Short ABC February 21st 210 Call	1 @ 7.10		
		Adjustment 3: Hold Puts , Long Call and Buy Back Short Call: ABC has risen 10 points from original entry point	
Hold the Long	1 @ 8.45	**New BP**: ($14.80 x 100) – ($19.10 x 100) + ($16.20 x 100) = $1190	**Profit**: $7.1 x 100 = $710
Hold Short Put	1 @ 4		
Hold Long Call	1 @ 24.90		
Buy Back Short Call	0		

Outcome: The adjustment capitalizes on full decay of the short call to 0. This yields an initial profit of $710. The price of the remaining options have changed and must be accounted for when making decisions about what to do next.

Risk / Reward Analysis: Remaining Risk and Possible Future Adjustments are determined by evaluating the remaining position. The Profit and Loss Graph for the remaining position is below.

Profit and Loss Graph after the Adjustment

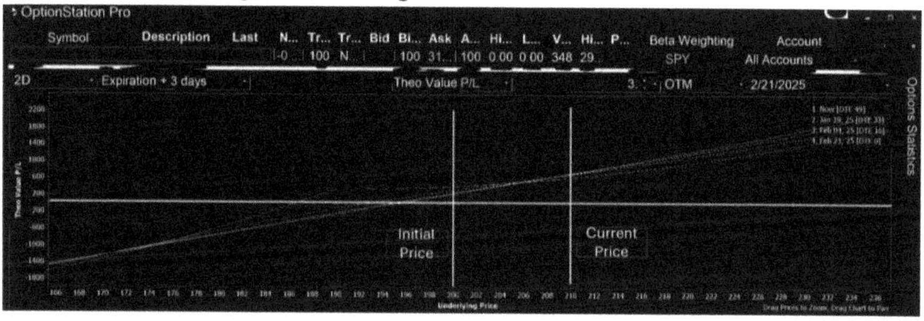

What to do Now? Possible Future Adjustments

With a profit in hand from the expired short call and now holding a long call and a bullish put diagonal the trader is in great shape if the underlying stock continues to move up. If the stock falters and appears to be ready for a pullback the trader can always reinstate the short call for a future month.

Example 1: Adjustment 4, Close the entire position

Scenario: **Scenario**: The underlying stock of a Batman Spread experiences a strong bullish rally and the stock price is now at 210.

Adjustment: The trader decides to close the entire position with a profit.

Position Characteristics At the Adjustment

Position	# of Options and Price	Buying Power (BP) Needed	Why Making Investment or Adjustment
Initial Batman Spread			
Long ABC August 15th 180 Put	1 @ 12.00	[($14.80 x 100 = $1480)] + [($19.10 x 100 = $1910)] = Total = $3390	Long options have slower decay than the short options, indicated by the lower Theta. Significant profit from decay in 1 month. The Theta will increase as options approach expiration.
Short ABC February 21st 190 Put	1 @ 7.20		
Long ABC August 15th 220 Call	1 @ 16.20		
Short ABC February 21st 210 Call	1 @ 7.10		
4. Close the Position Early: The short legs are expiring; the Underlying has risen 10 points from the original entry point.			
Sell the Long Put	0	**New BP:** N/A	**Profit:** [($12 - $8.45) + ($7.2 – 0) + ($24.50 – $16.20) + ($7.10 – $0)] x 100 = ($26.15 x 100) = $2615
Buy Back the Short Put	0		
Sell the Long Call	0		
Buy Back the Short Call	0		

Outcome: The adjustment capitalizes on the decay of the short positions to 0 and the smaller drop in the long-put price and gain in the long-call price. The total profit would be $2615.

D. Execution Plan:

Clear Action Steps: For each potential adjustment identified and ranked, develop clear, actionable steps for execution. This includes determining the optimal timing for making adjustments and any necessary preparatory actions.

Contingency Planning: Prepare for scenarios where the market moves against the position despite adjustments. This includes having predefined exit strategies or further adjustment options to mitigate losses.

Conclusion

Complex adjustments in Batman Spreads require a deep understanding of market dynamics, a keen sense of timing, and the strategic use of options mechanics. Through careful analysis and the judicious application of advanced adjustment strategies, traders can navigate market changes, harness volatility, and steer their positions toward optimal outcomes, demonstrating the art and science of campaign trading in the options realm.

5

Advanced Adjustment Strategies: Batman Spread Example 2

For the second Batman example shown in Chapter 2 a complete analysis using our tools and showing the outcomes is provided in the chapter.

A. Possible Adjustments for Example 2

The possible adjustments for this initial opening position based on market conditions are:

- Adjustment 1: Sell Long Put and Hold the Short Put and the Long and Short Calls
- Adjustment 2: Hold the Long Puts and Calls and Roll both Short Options
- Adjustment 3: Hold Puts and Long Calls and Buy Back Short Call

or

- Close the Position Early (prior to or at expiration of the short options)

B. Decision-Making Framework:

Decision Trees: Utilize decision trees to map out possible adjustment paths and their potential outcomes, providing a clear visual framework for decision-making.

Risk/Reward Analysis: Every potential adjustment should be evaluated in terms of its impact on the risk/reward profile of the position. This involves a thorough analysis of how adjustments might shift the risk exposure and potential returns.

Ranking Based on Probability of Success: Use historical data and analysis tools to rank potential adjustments by their likelihood of success, focusing on those with the highest probability of achieving the desired outcome.

The opening position and adjustment characteristics, including the Greeks, are shown for the 4 potential adjustment that we are evaluating.

Position Characteristics at the Adjustment and Outcomes

<table>
<tr><th>Position</th><th># of Options and Price</th><th>Buying Power (BP) Needed</th><th>Why Making Investment or Adjustment</th></tr>
<tr><td colspan="4">Initial Batman Spread</td></tr>
<tr><td>Long DEF July 18th 115 Put</td><td>2 @ 5.10</td><td rowspan="4">[($21.20 x 100 = $2120)] +
[($24.40 x 100 = $2440)] =
Total = $4560</td><td rowspan="4">Long options have slower decay than the short options, indicated by the lower Theta.
Significant profit from decay in 1 month. The Theta will increase as options approach expiration.</td></tr>
<tr><td>Short DEF February 7th 123 Put</td><td>2 @ 2.50</td></tr>
<tr><td>Long DEF July 18th 145 Call</td><td>2 @ 5.45</td></tr>
<tr><td>Short DEF February 7th 135 Call</td><td>2 @ 3.25</td></tr>
<tr><td colspan="4">Adjustment 1: Sell Long Put and Hold Short Put and Long and Short Calls :DEF has dropped 20 points from original entry</td></tr>
<tr><td>Sell Long Put</td><td>0 @ 22.30</td><td rowspan="2">New BP:</td><td rowspan="2">Profit: ($22.30 – $5.10) x 2 = $3440</td></tr>
<tr><td>Hold Short Put</td><td>2 @ 20.30</td></tr>
</table>

Hold Long Call	2 @ 2.20	($123 x 200 x 0.50) + [($5.45 - $3.25) x 200] + $2000 = $14740	4 months left for stock to recover.
Hold Short Put	2 @ 1.20		
Adjustment 2: Hold the Long Puts and Calls and Roll both Short Options : DEF has dropped 10 points from original entry			
Hold Long Put	2 @ 17.30	**New BP**: {[($5.10 – 10.80) + ($3.25 – 2.10)] x 2 x 100} + [($800 + $1000) x 2] = $2690	**Profit:** [(-$4 + $2.50) x 2 x 100] + ($3.25 x 2 x 100) = $350 Not much decay after 1 month
Roll Short Puts	2 @ 10.80		
Hold Long Calls	2 @ 3.45		
Roll Short Calls	2 @ 2.10		
Adjustment 3: Hold Puts, Long Call and Buy Back Short Call.DEF has risen 10 points from original entry point			
Hold Long Put	2 @ 2.8	**New BP**: [($5.10 -$2.50) x 2 x 100] + $1600 + ($5.45 x 2 x 100) = $3628	**Loss**: ($3.25 – $4.00) x 2 x 100 = $150.
Hold Short Puts	2 @ 1.50		
Hold Long Calls	2 @ 7.80		
Buy Back Short Calls	0 @ 6.45		
4.Close Position: The Underlying has risen 10 points from the original entry point.			
Sell Long Puts	0	**New BP**:	

<table>
<tr><td>Buy Back Short Puts</td><td>0</td><td rowspan="3">N/A</td><td rowspan="3">Profit: [($5.10 -$2.8) + ($2.50) + ($7.80 – $5.45) + ($3.25 – $6.45)] x 2 x 100 = $790</td></tr>
<tr><td>Sell Long Calls</td><td>0</td></tr>
<tr><td>Buy Back Short Calls</td><td>0</td></tr>
</table>

Notes:

1) 50% Margin,

2) The Buying Power (BP) Needed column depicts Buying Power for the adjusted position and not the change to the Buying Power.

C. **Systematic Response**: According to the decision-making framework, the trader evaluates each of the adjustments to determine the best choice for a specific moment.

Example 2: Adjustment 1, Sell Long Put and Hold the Short Put and the Long and Short Calls

Scenario: The underlying diversified industrials products solution company stock of a Batman Spread experiences a strong bearish move dropping 20 points to 109.

Adjustment: The trader sells the long call leg at a profit and holds the remainder of the position.

Position Characteristics At the Adjustment

Position	# of Options and Price	Buying Power (BP) Needed	Why Making Investment or Adjustment
Initial Batman Spread			
Long DEF July 18th 115 Put	2 @ 5.10	[($21.20 x 100 = $2120)] + [($24.40 x 100 = $2440)] = Total = $4560	Long options have slower decay than the short options, indicated by the lower Theta. Significant profit from decay in 1 month. The Theta will increase as options approach expiration.
Short DEF February 7th 123 Put	2 @ 2.50		
Long DEF July 18th 145 Call	2 @ 5.45		
Short DEF February 7th 135 Call	2 @ 3.25		
Adjustment 1: Sell Long Put and Hold Short Put and Long and Short Calls : DEF has dropped 20 points from original entry			
Sell Long Put	0 @ 22.30	**New BP**: ($123 x 200 x 0.50) + [($5.45 - $3.25) x 200] + $2000 = $14740	**Profit**: ($22.30 – $5.10) x 2 = $3440 4 months left for stock to recover.
Hold Short Put	2 @ 20.30		
Hold Long Call	2 @ 2.20		
Hold Short Put	2 @ 1.20		

Outcome: The adjustment capitalizes on the increased volatility and in the money increasing delta of the long leg to extract higher premiums and profits of $3440.

Risk / Reward Analysis: Remaining Risk and Possible Future Adjustments are determined by evaluating the remaining position. The Profit and Loss Graph for the remaining position is below.

Profit and Loss Graph after the Adjustment

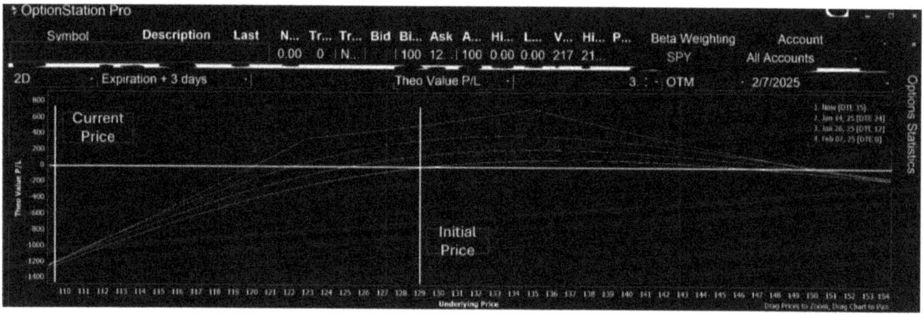

If the stock rises to above the strike price of the short leg, the trader can recover the entire value of the remaining short leg. But if the stock continues to fall the loss can mount.

What to do Now? Possible Future Adjustments

With a profit in hand and a remaining short put and bearish call diagonal, the trader will benefit if the underlying stock moves back to the initial price or at least within the range that indicates a profit on the revised Profit and Loss graph. One possible way to manage this situation is to roll the short calls when the premium is decayed to the next month or a few weeks just to keep the position alive and to keep making the premium and maintain this until the stock moves back up.

Example 2: Adjustment 2, Hold the Long Puts and Calls and Roll both Short Options

Scenario: The underlying stock of a Batman Spread drops 10 points to 119. When the short options expire, the trader can choose to close the position for a profit or to roll the shorts to a future expiration date. This can continue until the long options expire.

Adjustment: The trader rolls the short options to the same or different strike, extending the expiration to capture additional premium.

Position Characteristics At the Adjustment

<table>
<tr><th>Position</th><th># of Options and Price</th><th>Buying Power (BP) Needed</th><th>Why Making Investment or Adjustment</th></tr>
<tr><td colspan="4">Initial Batman Spread</td></tr>
<tr><td>Long DEF July 18th 115 Put</td><td>2 @ 5.10</td><td rowspan="4">[($21.20 x 100 = $2120)] +
[($24.40 x 100 = $2440)] =
Total = $4560</td><td rowspan="4">Long options have slower decay than the short options, indicated by the lower Theta.
Significant profit from decay in 1 month. The Theta will increase as options approach expiration.</td></tr>
<tr><td>Short DEF February 7th 123 Put</td><td>2 @ 2.50</td></tr>
<tr><td>Long DEF July 18th 145 Call</td><td>2 @ 5.45</td></tr>
<tr><td>Short DEF February 7th 135 Call</td><td>2 @ 3.25</td></tr>
<tr><td colspan="4">Adjustment 2: Hold the Long Puts and Calls and Roll both Short Options : DEF has dropped 10 points from original entry</td></tr>
<tr><td>Hold Long Put</td><td>2 @ 17.30</td><td rowspan="4">New BP:
{[($5.10 – 10.80) + ($3.25 – 2.10)] x 2 x 100} + [($800 + $1000) x 2] = $2690</td><td rowspan="4">Profit: [(-$4 + $2.50) x 2 x 100] + ($3.25 x 2 x 100) = $350
Not much decay after 1 month</td></tr>
<tr><td>Roll Short Puts</td><td>2 @ 10.80</td></tr>
<tr><td>Hold Long Calls</td><td>2 @ 3.45</td></tr>
<tr><td>Roll Short Calls</td><td>2 @ 2.10</td></tr>
</table>

Outcome: The adjustment capitalizes on the complete decay of the short options to zero premiums. The long legs have experienced limited decay. The rolling of the short puts and calls yields a total profit of $350.

Risk / Reward Analysis: Remaining Risk and Possible Future Adjustments are determined by evaluating the remaining position. The Profit and Loss Graph for the remaining position is shown below.

Profit and Loss Graph after the Adjustment

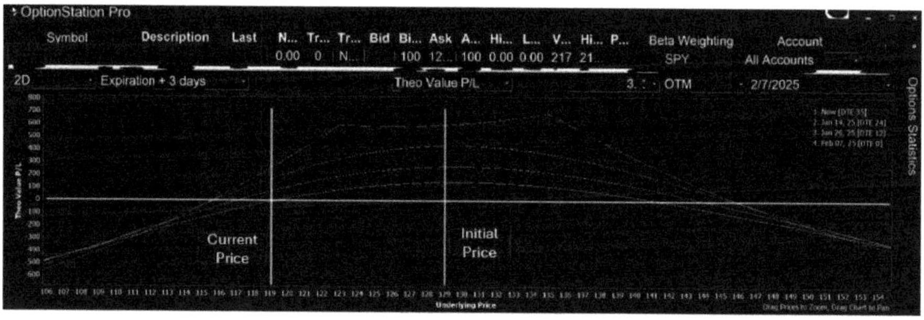

What to do Now? Possible Future Adjustments

With a small profit in hand from the expired short put, the trader will benefit if the underlying stock stays close to the same price or moves back up. One possible way to manage this scenario is to continue to roll the shorts when the premium is decayed out to the next month or a few weeks just to keep the position alive and to keep making the premium until the long legs approach expiration.

Example 2: Adjustment 3, Hold Puts and Long Calls and Buy Back Short Call

Scenario: The underlying stock of a Batman Spread experiences a strong bullish rally and the price is now at 139.

Adjustment: The trader holds the long and short puts and the long calls and buys back the short calls. DEF has risen 10 points from original entry point

Position Characteristics At the Adjustment

Position	# of Options and Price	Buying Power (BP) Needed	Why Making Investment or Adjustment
Initial Batman Spread			
Long DEF July 18th 115 Put	2 @ 5.10	[($21.20 x 100 = $2120)] + [($24.40 x 100 = $2440)] = Total = $4560	Long options have slower decay than the short options, indicated by the lower Theta. Significant profit from decay in 1 month. The Theta will increase as options approach expiration.
DEF February 7th 123 Put	2 @ 2.50		
Long DEF July 18th 145 Call	2 @ 5.45		
Short DEF February 7th 135 Call	2 @ 3.25		
Adjustment 3: Hold Puts, Long Call and Buy Back Short Call.DEF has risen 10 points from original entry point			
Hold Long Put	2 @ 2.8	**New BP**: [($5.10 -$2.50) x 2 x 100] + $1600 + ($5.45 x 2 x 100) = $3628	**Loss**: ($3.25 – $4.00) x 2 x 100 = $150.
Hold Short Puts	2 @ 1.50		
Hold Long Calls	2 @ 7.80		
Buy Back Short Calls	0 @ 6.45		

Outcome: The adjustment capitalizes on the decay of the short calls to $4. This yields an initial loss of $150 from the short call. The price of the long put has dropped to $2.80 and the long call has risen in price to $7.80.

Risk / Reward Analysis: Remaining Risk and Possible Future Adjustments are determined by evaluating the remaining position. The Profit and Loss Graph for the remaining position is shown below.

Profit and Loss Graph after the Adjustment

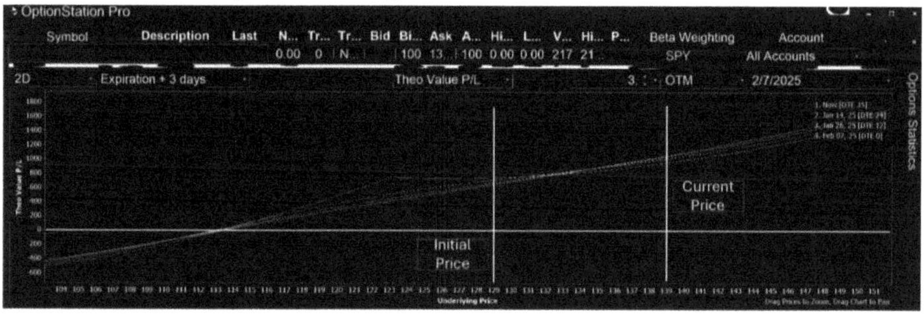

What to do Now? Possible Future Adjustments

With a small loss in hand from the expired short put and now holding a long call and bullish put diagonal that is OTM, the trader will benefit if the underlying stock continues to moves up. The trader may decide to hold the put diagonal for a short time watching to see what the underlying stock does.

Example 2: Adjustment 4, Close the entire position

Scenario: **Scenario**: The underlying stock of a Batman Spread experiences a strong bullish rally and the stock price is now at 139.

Adjustment: The trader decides to close the entire position with a profit.

Position Characteristics At the Adjustment

<table>
<tr><th>Position</th><th># of Options and Price</th><th>Buying Power (BP) Needed</th><th>Why Making Investment or Adjustment</th></tr>
<tr><td colspan="4">Initial Batman Spread</td></tr>
<tr><td>Long DEF July 18th 115 Put</td><td>2 @ 5.10</td><td rowspan="4">[($21.20 x 100 = $2120)] +
[($24.40 x 100 = $2440)] =
Total = $4560</td><td rowspan="4">Long options have slower decay than the short options, indicated by the lower Theta.
Significant profit from decay in 1 month. The Theta will increase as options approach expiration.</td></tr>
<tr><td>Short DEF February 7th 123 Put</td><td>2 @ 2.50</td></tr>
<tr><td>Long DEF July 18th 145 Call</td><td>2 @ 5.45</td></tr>
<tr><td>Short DEF February 7th 135 Call</td><td>2 @ 3.25</td></tr>
<tr><td colspan="4">4.Close Position: The Underlying has risen 10 points from the original entry point.</td></tr>
<tr><td>Sell Long Puts</td><td>0</td><td rowspan="4">New BP:
N/A</td><td rowspan="4">Profit: [($5.10 -$2.8) + ($2.50) + ($7.80 – $5.45) + ($3.25 – $6.45)] x 2 x 100 = $790</td></tr>
<tr><td>Buy Back Short Puts</td><td>0</td></tr>
<tr><td>Sell Long Calls</td><td>0</td></tr>
<tr><td>Buy Back Short Calls</td><td>0</td></tr>
</table>

Outcome: The adjustment capitalizes on the decay of the short positions to 0 and smaller drops in the long options. The total profit would be $790.

D. Execution Plan:

Clear Action Steps: For each potential adjustment identified and ranked, develop clear, actionable steps for execution. This includes determining the optimal timing for making adjustments and any necessary preparatory actions.

Contingency Planning: Prepare for scenarios where the market moves against the position despite adjustments. This includes having predefined exit strategies or further adjustment options to mitigate losses.

Conclusion

Complex adjustments in Batman Spreads require a deep understanding of market dynamics, a keen sense of timing, and the strategic use of options mechanics. Through careful analysis and the judicious application of advanced adjustment strategies, traders can navigate market changes, harness volatility, and steer their positions toward optimal outcomes, demonstrating the art and science of campaign trading in the options realm.

6

Advanced Adjustment Strategies: Calendar Spread Example 1

For the first Calendar example shown in Chapter 2 we will provide a complete analysis using our tools and show the outcomes in this chapter.

A. Possible Adjustments for Example 1

There are numerous possible adjustments for this initial opening position based on market conditions but for our purposes we will evaluate these:

- Adjustment 1: Sell Long and Hold Short
- Adjustment 2: Hold Long and Roll Short
- Adjustment 3: Hold Long and Buy Back Short

or

- Close the Position Early (prior to or at expiration of the short put)

B. Decision-Making Framework:

Decision Trees: Utilize decision trees to map out possible adjustment paths and their potential outcomes, providing a clear visual framework for decision-making.

Risk/Reward Analysis: Every potential adjustment should be evaluated in terms of its impact on the risk/reward profile of the position. This involves a thorough analysis of how adjustments might shift the risk exposure and potential returns.

Ranking Based on Probability of Success: Use historical data and analysis tools to rank potential adjustments by their likelihood of success, focusing on those with the highest probability of achieving the desired outcome. Before we do our analysis let's see what ChatGPT can offer.

Prompt

As an expert options trader please describe the best market environment and anticipated movement of the underlying stock for the use of a Calendar Spread composed of 2 ea. Long XYZ August 15th 230 Put at a price of $21.30 and 2 ea. Short XYZ February 21st 230 Put at a price of $12.30. Please describe the various stock movements after open and rank the most likely stock movement to yield the trader with a profit. The trade is opened January 2nd when the stock is trading at a price of 226 with a volatility of 0.3139.

Response with ChatGPT

A Calendar Spread, in this case composed of 2 long-dated August 15th 230 Puts and 2 short-dated February 21st 230 Puts, is a strategy designed to benefit from time decay (theta) and implied volatility (vega) dynamics. Here is a breakdown of the best market environment, anticipated stock movements, and profitability scenarios:

Best Market Environment for the Calendar Spread: Stable Market with Minimal Price Movement

The Calendar Spread profits most when the stock price remains close to the strike price ($230) until the expiration of the short-dated February 21st options.

This maximizes the time decay of the short options, while the long options retain their time value due to their later expiration date.

Moderate to Increasing Implied Volatility: Implied volatility (IV) plays a significant role in Calendar Spreads. An increase in IV benefits the long-dated August options, as their value is more sensitive to changes in volatility compared to the shorter-dated February options.

Neutral Delta:

This trade is delta-neutral at initiation, meaning it has little directional bias. However, it becomes slightly directional if the stock moves significantly away from $230.

Analysis of Stock Movements

1. Stock Stays Near $230 Until February 21st (Ideal Scenario)

Outcome: This is the most profitable scenario.

The February 21st short puts decay faster, eventually expiring worthless.

The August 15th long puts retain significant time value, as they have more than 170 days remaining until expiration.

Time decay (theta) works in favor of the trade, and any increase in implied volatility further enhances the long options' value.

Profitability: High.

2. Stock Moves Slightly Above $230 Before February 21st

Outcome: Moderately profitable.

If the stock drifts slightly above $230, the February short puts still lose value quickly due to time decay.

The long puts retain some value because the stock is still near the strike price and has significant time to expiration.

Profitability: Moderate.

3. Stock Moves Slightly Below $230 Before February 21st

Outcome: Similar to the previous scenario, moderately profitable.

If the stock drifts slightly below $230, the February short puts lose value as they approach expiration, while the August long puts gain some intrinsic value.

However, if the stock drops too far, the short puts may gain intrinsic value faster than expected, which could offset some gains.

Profitability: Moderate.

4. Stock Drops Significantly Below $230

Outcome: Potential loss or breakeven.

A sharp decline below $230 results in the February short puts gaining significant intrinsic value, causing losses that could offset the gains from the August long puts.

This scenario is undesirable because the spread becomes delta-negative, making it sensitive to further declines.

Profitability: Low.

5. Stock Rises Significantly Above $230

Outcome: Limited profit or breakeven.

If the stock rises significantly above $230, both the February short puts and the August long puts lose value.

The short puts decay faster, but the long puts retain little extrinsic value, resulting in minimal gains or small losses.

Profitability: Low to Moderate.

Ranking the Scenarios for Profitability

Stock remains near $230 until February 21st: Most profitable due to maximized time decay of the short options and retention of value in the long options.

Stock moves slightly above or below $230: Moderately profitable because time decay still benefits the trade, though intrinsic value changes slightly offset gains.

Stock rises significantly above $230: Limited profit because the short options decay, but the long options lose extrinsic value.

Stock drops significantly below $230: Least profitable due to increased intrinsic value of the short options, potentially leading to losses.

Key Considerations

Time Decay (Theta): The Calendar Spread relies on the faster decay of the February short puts relative to the August long puts. Holding the position close to expiration maximizes this effect.

Implied Volatility (Vega): An increase in IV benefits the trade, as the August long puts are more sensitive to volatility changes than the February short puts. A decrease in IV can reduce the spread's value, making it less profitable.

Directional Bias (Delta): The trade starts delta-neutral, but a significant move in the underlying stock creates a directional exposure. The closer the stock remains to $230, the better the trade performs.

Summary

This Calendar Spread is best suited for a neutral market environment with moderate or rising volatility. The most profitable scenario occurs when the stock price remains close to $230 until February 21st, allowing the short options to decay while the long options retain value. Traders should monitor implied volatility and stock movement to adjust the position if necessary.

The opening position and adjustment characteristics, including the Greeks, are shown for the 4 potential adjustment that we are evaluating.

Position Characteristics at the Adjustment and Outcomes

Position	# of Options and Price	Buying Power (BP) Needed	Why Making Investment or Adjustment
Initial Calendar Spread			
Long XYZ August 15th 230 Put	2 @ 21.30	$9 x 100 = $900 x 2 = $1800	Slower decay than the short put, indicated by the lower Theta.
Short XYZ February 21st 230 Put	2 @ 12.30		Significant profit from decay in 1 month. The Theta will increase as options approach expiration.
Adjustment 1: Sell Long and Hold Short: XYZ has dropped 20 points from original entry point			
Sell the Long	0 @ 41.10	**New BP**	**Profit**: $1980 x 2 = $3960
Hold the Short	2 @ 42.00	230 x 2 x 100 x 0.5 = $23,000	5 months left for stock to recover.
Adjustment 2: Hold Long and Roll Short: XYZ has dropped 10 points from original entry point			
Hold Long	2 @ 31.10	**New BP**:	Not much decay after 1 month
Roll Short	2 @ 17.85	($21.30 – $17.85) x 2 x 100 = $690	**Loss**: ($12.30 – $14.00) x 2 x 100 = $340
Adjustment 3: Hold Long and Buy Back Short: XYZ has risen 10 points from original entry point			
Hold the Long	2 @ 12.80	**New BP**:	Anticipating a drop in stock price.

Buy Back the Short	0	($21.30 x 2 x 100) = $4260	**Profit**: $12.30 x 2 x 100 = $2460
4. Close Position: The short leg has expired or the Underlying has risen 10 points from the original entry point.			
Sell the Long	0	**New BP:** **N/A**	**Loss**: $850 x 2 = $1700
Buy Back the Short	0		**Profit**: $1230 x 2 = $2460
Total Profit: $2460 - $1700 = $760			

Notes:

1) 50% Margin,

2) The Buying Power (BP) Needed column depicts Buying Power for the adjusted position and not the change to the Buying Power.

C. Systematic Response: According to the decision-making framework, the trader evaluates each of the adjustments to determine the best choice for a specific moment.

Decision Tree: Mapped out below for this example.

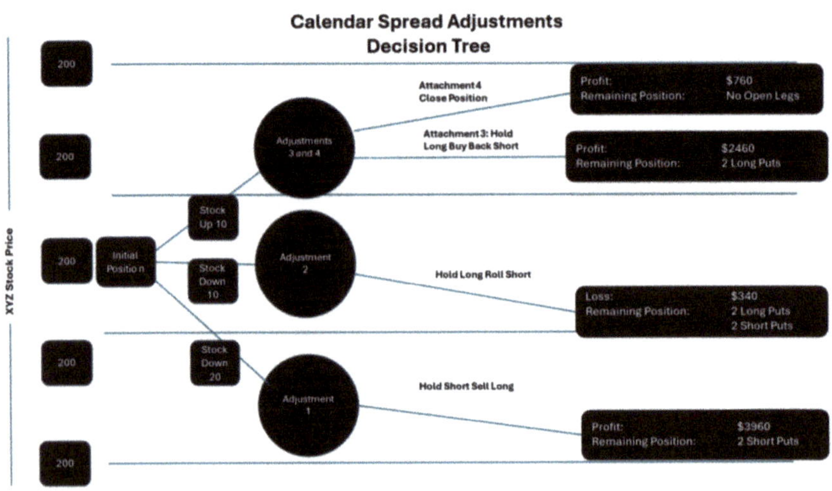

Example 1: Adjustment 1, Sell Long and Hold Short

Scenario: The underlying stock of a Calendar Spread experiences a strong bearish move dropping 20 points to 206.

Adjustment: The trader sells the long leg at a profit and holds the short leg.

Position Characteristics At the Adjustment

Position	# of Options and Price	Buying Power (BP) Needed	Why Making Investment or Adjustment
Initial Calendar Spread			
Long XYZ August 15th 230 Put	2 @ 21.30	$9 x 100 = $900 x 2 = $1800	Slower decay than the short put, indicated by the lower Theta.
Short XYZ February 21st 230 Put	2 @ 12.30		Significant profit from decay in 1 month. The Theta will increase as options approach expiration.
Adjustment 1: Sell Long and Hold Short: XYZ has dropped 20 points from original entry point			
Sell the Long	0 @ 41.10	**New BP**	**Profit**: $1980 x 2 = $3960
Hold the Short	2 @ 42.00	230 x 2 x 100 x 0.5 = $23,000	5 months left for stock to recover.

Outcome: The adjustment capitalizes on the increased volatility and in the money increasing delta of the long leg to extract higher premiums and profits of $3960.

Risk / Reward Analysis: Remaining Risk and Possible Future Adjustments are determined by evaluating the remaining position. The Profit and Loss Graph for the remaining position is below.

Profit and Loss Graph after the Adjustment

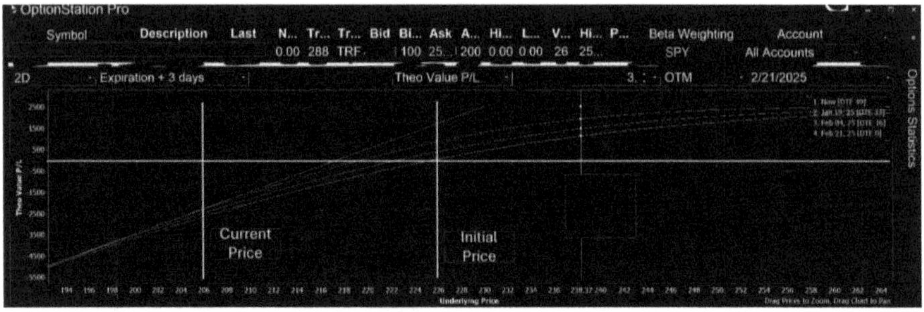

If the stock rises to above the strike price of the short leg, the trader can recover the entire value of the remaining short leg. But if the stock continues to fall the loss can mount.

What to do Now? Possible Future Adjustments

With a profit in hand and a remaining short put, the trader will benefit if the underlying stock moves back to the strike price of the short put. One possible way to manage this situation is to roll the short when the premium is decayed to the next month or a few weeks just to keep the position alive and to keep making the premium and maintain this until the stock moves back up.

Example 1: Adjustment 2, Hold Long and Roll Short

Scenario: The underlying stock of a Calendar Spread drops 10 points to 216. When the short put expires, the trader can choose to close the position for a profit or to roll the short put to a future expiration date. This can continue until the long put expires.

Adjustment: The trader rolls the short put to the same or higher strike, extending the expiration to capture additional premium.

Position Characteristics At the Adjustment

Position	# of Options and Price	Buying Power (BP) Needed	Why Making Investment or Adjustment
Initial Calendar Spread			
Long XYZ August 15th 230 Put	2 @ 21.30	$9 x 100 = $900 x 2 = $1800	Slower decay than the short put, indicated by the lower Theta.
Short XYZ February 21st 230 Put	2 @ 12.30		Significant profit from decay in 1 month. The Theta will increase as options approach expiration.
Adjustment 2: Hold Long and Roll Short: XYZ has dropped 10 points from original entry point			
Hold Long	2 @ 31.10	**New BP**: ($21.30 – $17.85) x 2 x 100 = $690	Not much decay after 1 month
Roll Short	2 @ 17.85		**Loss**: ($12.30 – $14.00) x 2 x 100 = $340

Outcome: The adjustment capitalizes on the complete decay of the short put to zero premium but the intrinsic value of the short leg is now 14 because the stock has dropped 10 points to 216. The long has experienced limited decay. The rolling of the short put yields an initial loss of $340, assuming that the short put expires to $0 premium and has an intrinsic value of 14.

Risk / Reward Analysis: Remaining Risk and Possible Future Adjustments are determined by evaluating the remaining position. The Profit and Loss Graph for the remaining position is below.

Profit and Loss Graph after the Adjustment

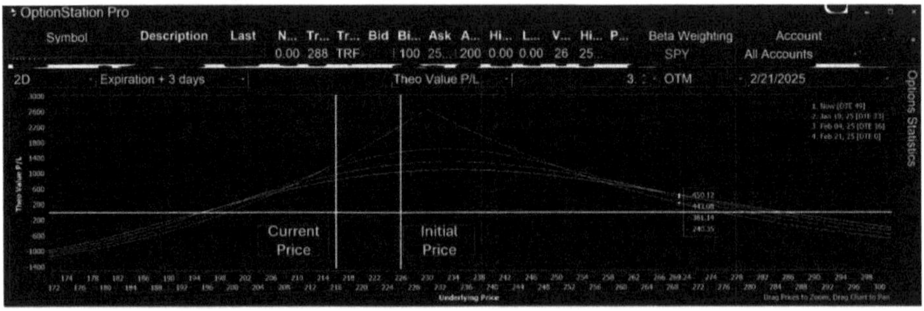

What to do Now? Possible Future Adjustments

With a small loss in hand from the expired short put, the trader will benefit if the underlying stock stays close to the same price or moves back up. One possible way to manage this scenario is to continue to roll the short when the premium is decayed out to the next month or a few weeks just to keep the position alive and to keep making the premium until the long-put approaches expiration.

Example 1: Adjustment 3, Hold Long and Buy Back Short

Scenario: The underlying stock of a Calendar Spread experiences a strong bullish rally and the price is now at 236.

Adjustment: The trader buys back the short and holds the long put.

Position Characteristics At the Adjustment

Position	# of Options and Price	Buying Power (BP) Needed	Why Making Investment or Adjustment
Initial Calendar Spread			
Long XYZ August 15th 230 Put	2 @ 21.30	$9 x 100 = $900 x 2 = $1800	Slower decay than the short put, indicated by the lower Theta.
Short XYZ February 21st 230 Put	2 @ 12.30		Significant profit from decay in 1 month. The Theta will increase as options approach expiration.
Adjustment 3: Hold Long and Buy Back Short: XYZ has risen 10 points from original entry point			
Hold the Long	2 @ 12.80	**New BP**: ($21.30 x 2 x 100) = $4260	Anticipating a drop in stock price.
Buy Back the Short	0		**Profit**: $12.30 x 2 x 100 = $2460

Outcome: The adjustment capitalizes on full decay of the short put to 0. This yields an initial profit of $2460 from the short puts. The price of the long put has dropped to 12.80.

Risk / Reward Analysis: Remaining Risk and Possible Future Adjustments are determined by evaluating the remaining position. The Profit and Loss Graph for the remaining position is below.

Profit and Loss Graph after the Adjustment

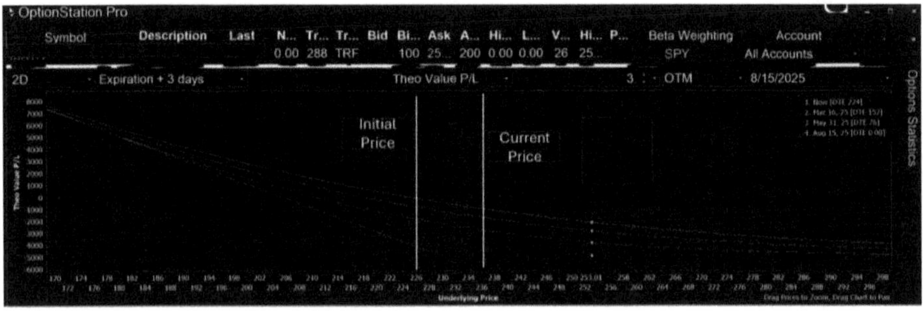

What to do Now? Possible Future Adjustments

With a profit in hand from the expired short put and now holding a long put the is 10 points OTM, the trader will benefit if the underlying stock moves down a lot. The trader may decide to hold the put for a short time watching to see what the underlying stock does. The odds are low that the stock would move enough to make the long put profitable but the trader may decide to sell the short put again and the same or higher strike price if the stock does come down some.

Example 1: Adjustment 4, Close the entire position

Scenario: **Scenario**: The underlying stock of a Calendar Spread experiences a strong bullish rally and the stock price is now at 236.

Adjustment: The trader decides to close the entire position with a profit.

Position Characteristics At the Adjustment

Position	# of Options and Price	Buying Power (BP) Needed	Why Making Investment or Adjustment
Initial Calendar Spread			
Long XYZ August 15th 230 Put	2 @ 21.30	$9 x 100 = $900 x 2 = $1800	Slower decay than the short put, indicated by the lower Theta.
Short XYZ February 21st 230 Put	2 @ 12.30		Significant profit from decay in 1 month. The Theta will increase as options approach expiration.
4. Close Position: The short leg has expired or the Underlying has risen 10 points from the original entry point.			
Sell the Long	0	**New BP:** N/A	**Loss**: $850 x 2 = $1700
Buy Back the Short	0		**Profit**: $1230 x 2 = $2460
Total Profit: $2460 - $1700 = $760			

Outcome: The adjustment capitalizes on the decay of the short position to 0 and the smaller drop in the long-put price. The total profit would be $2460 - $1700 = $760.

D. Execution Plan:

Clear Action Steps: For each potential adjustment identified and ranked, develop clear, actionable steps for execution. This includes determining the optimal timing for making adjustments and any necessary preparatory actions.

Contingency Planning: Prepare for scenarios where the market moves against the position despite adjustments. This includes having predefined exit strategies or further adjustment options to mitigate losses.

Conclusion

Complex adjustments in Calendar Spreads require a deep understanding of market dynamics, a keen sense of timing, and the strategic use of options mechanics. Through careful analysis and the judicious application of advanced adjustment strategies, traders can navigate market changes, harness volatility, and steer their positions toward optimal outcomes, demonstrating the art and science of campaign trading in the options realm.

7

Advanced Adjustment Strategies: Calendar Spread Example 2

For the second Calendar example shown in Chapter 2 we will provide a complete analysis using our tools and show the outcomes in the chapter.

A. Possible Adjustments for Example 2

The possible adjustments for this initial opening position based on market conditions are:

- Adjustment 1: Sell Long and Hold Short
- Adjustment 2: Hold Long and Roll Short
- Adjustment 3: Buy Back Short and Hold Long

or

- Close the Position Early or at expiration

B. Decision-Making Framework:

Decision Trees: Utilize decision trees to map out possible adjustment paths and their potential outcomes, providing a clear visual framework for decision-making.

Risk/Reward Analysis: Every potential adjustment should be evaluated in terms of its impact on the risk/reward profile of the position. This involves a thorough analysis of how adjustments might shift the risk exposure and potential returns.

Ranking Based on Probability of Success: Use historical data and analysis tools to rank potential adjustments by their likelihood of success, focusing on those with the highest probability of achieving the desired outcome.

The opening position and adjustment characteristics, including the Greeks, are shown for the 4 potential adjustment that we are evaluating.

Position Characteristics at the Adjustment and Outcomes

Position	# of Options and Price	Buying Power (BP) Needed	Why Making Investment or Adjustment
Initial Calendar Spread			
Long UVW July 18th 135 Put	3 @ 29.10	$12.10 x 3 x 100 = $3630	Slower decay than the short put, indicated by the lower Theta.
Short UVW February 21st 135 Put	3 @ 17.00		Significant profit from decay in 1 month. The Theta will increase as options approach expiration.
Adjustment 1: Sell Long and Hold Short: UVW has dropped 20 points from original entry point			
Sell the Long	0 @ 48.90	**New BP**: $135 x 3 100 x 0.50 = $20,250	**Profit**: $1980 x 3 = $5940
Hold the Short	3 @ 30.00		3 months left for stock to recover.
Adjustment 2: Hold Long and Roll Short: UVW has dropped 10 points from original entry point			
Hold Long	3 @ 38.90	**New BP**: $(29.10 – 25.00) x 3 x 100 = $1230	Not much decay after 1 month
Roll Short	3 @ 25.00		**Profit:** ($17.00 – $13.00) x 3 x 100 = $1200
Adjustment 3: Hold Long and Buy Back Short. UVW has risen 10 points from original entry point			

<table>
<tr><td>Hold the Long</td><td>3 @ 23.90</td><td rowspan="2">New BP:
$29.10 x 3 x 100 =
$8730</td><td>Anticipating a drop in stock price.</td></tr>
<tr><td>Buy Back the Short</td><td>0</td><td>Profit: 17.00 x 3 x 100 = $5100.</td></tr>
<tr><td colspan="4">4.Close Position: The short leg has expired or the Underlying has risen 10 points from the original entry point.</td></tr>
<tr><td>Sell the Long</td><td>0 @ 23.90</td><td rowspan="2">New BP:
N/A</td><td>Loss: $(29.10 – 23.90) x 3 x 100 = $1560</td></tr>
<tr><td>Buy Back the Short</td><td>0</td><td>Profit: $17 x 3 x 100 =
$5100</td></tr>
<tr><td colspan="4">Total Profit: -$5100 + $1560 = $3540</td></tr>
</table>

Notes:

1) 50% Margin,

2) The Buying Power (BP) Needed column depicts Buying Power for the adjusted position and not the change to the Buying Power.

C. **Systematic Response**: According to the decision-making framework, the trader evaluates each of the adjustments to determine the best choice for a specific moment.

Example 2: Adjustment 1, Sell Long and Hold Short

Scenario: The underlying semiconductor solution company's stock of a Calendar Spread experiences a strong bearish move dropping 20 points to 112.

Adjustment: The trader sells the long leg at a profit and holds the short leg.

Position Characteristics At the Adjustment

Position	# of Options and Price	Buying Power (BP) Needed	Why Making Investment or Adjustment
Initial Calendar Spread			
Long UVW July 18th 135 Put	3 @ 29.10	$12.10 x 3 x 100 = $3630	Slower decay than the short put, indicated by the lower Theta.
Short UVW February 21st 135 Put	3 @ 17.00		Significant profit from decay in 1 month. The Theta will increase as options approach expiration.
Adjustment 1: Sell Long and Hold Short:UVW has dropped 20 points from original entry point			
Sell the Long	0 @ 48.90	**New BP**: $135 x 3 x 100 x 0.50 = $20,250	**Profit**: $1980 x 3 = $5940
Hold the Short	3 @ 30.00		3 months left for stock to recover.

Outcome: The adjustment capitalizes on the increased volatility and in the money increasing delta of the long leg to extract higher premiums and profits of $5940.

Risk / Reward Analysis: Remaining Risk and Possible Future Adjustments are determined by evaluating the remaining position. The Profit and Loss Graph for the remaining position is below.

Profit and Loss Graph after the Adjustment

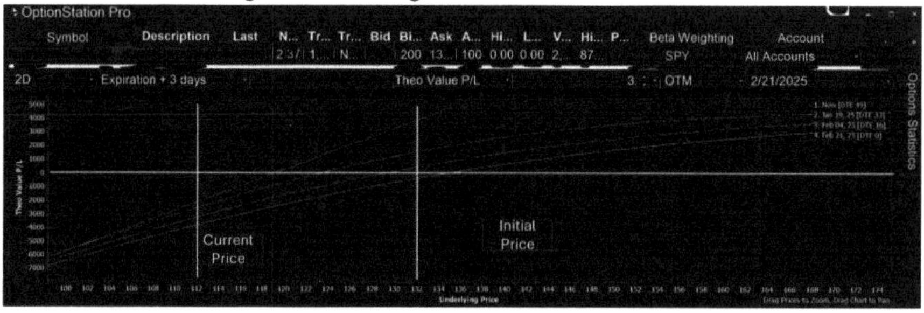

If the stock rises to above the strike price of the short leg, the trader can recover the entire value of the remaining short leg. But if the stock continues to fall the loss can mount.

What to do Now? Possible Future Adjustments

With a profit in hand and a remaining short put, the trader will benefit if the underlying stock moves back to the strike price of the short put. One possible way to manage this situation is to roll the short when the premium is decayed to the next month or a few weeks just to keep the position alive and to keep making the premium and maintain this until the stock moves back up.

Example 2: Adjustment 2, Hold Long and Roll Short

Scenario: The underlying stock of a Calendar Spread drops 10 points to 122. When the short put expires, the trader can choose to close the position for a profit or to roll the short put to a future expiration date. This can continue until the long put expires.

Adjustment: The trader rolls the short put to the same or higher strike, extending the expiration to capture additional premium.

Position Characteristics At the Adjustment

<table>
<tr><th>Position</th><th># of Options and Price</th><th>Buying Power (BP) Needed</th><th>Why Making Investment or Adjustment</th></tr>
<tr><td colspan="4">Initial Calendar Spread</td></tr>
<tr><td>Long UVW July 18th 135 Put</td><td>3 @ 29.10</td><td rowspan="2">$12.10 x 3 x 100 = $3630</td><td>Slower decay than the short put, indicated by the lower Theta.</td></tr>
<tr><td>Short UVW February 21st 135 Put</td><td>3 @ 17.00</td><td>Significant profit from decay in 1 month. The Theta will increase as options approach expiration.</td></tr>
<tr><td colspan="4">Adjustment 2: Hold Long and Roll Short: UVW has dropped 10 points from original entry point</td></tr>
<tr><td>Hold Long</td><td>3 @ 38.90</td><td rowspan="2">New BP:
$(29.10 – 25.00) x 3 x 100 = $1230</td><td>Not much decay after 1 month</td></tr>
<tr><td>Roll Short</td><td>3 @ 25.00</td><td>Profit: ($17.00 – $13.00) x 3 x 100 = $1200</td></tr>
</table>

Outcome: The adjustment capitalizes on the complete decay of the short put to zero premium but the intrinsic value of the short leg is now 10 because the stock has dropped 10 points to 122. The long has experienced limited decay. The rolling of the short put yields an initial profit of $1200, assuming that the short put expires to $0 premium and has an intrinsic value of 13.

Risk / Reward Analysis: Remaining Risk and Possible Future Adjustments are determined by evaluating the remaining position. The Profit and Loss Graph for the remaining position is shown below.

Profit and Loss Graph after the Adjustment

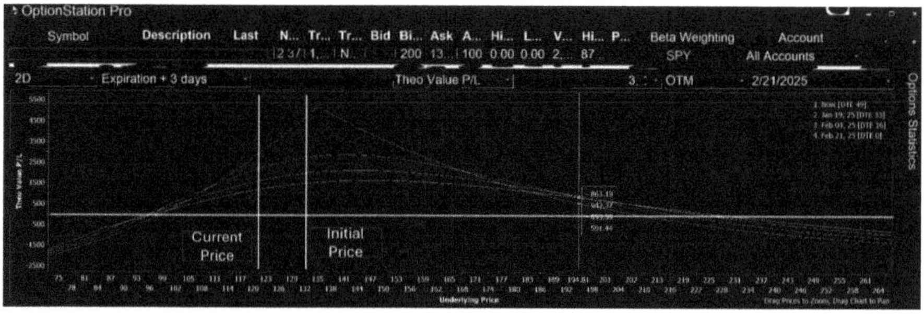

What to do Now? Possible Future Adjustments

With a small profit in hand from the expired short put, the trader will benefit if the underlying stock stays close to the same price or moves back up. One possible way to manage this scenario is to continue to roll the short when the premium is decayed to the next month or a few weeks just to keep the position alive and to keep making the premium until the long-put approaches expiration.

Example 2: Adjustment 3, Hold Long and Buy Back Short

Scenario: The underlying stock of a Calendar Spread experiences a strong bullish rally and the price is now at 142.

Adjustment: The trader buys back the short and holds the long put.

Position Characteristics At the Adjustment

Position	# of Options and Price	Buying Power (BP) Needed	Why Making Investment or Adjustment
Initial Calendar Spread			
Long UVW July 18th 135 Put	3 @ 29.10	$12.10 x 3 x 100 = $3630	Slower decay than the short put, indicated by the lower Theta.
Short UVW February 21st 135 Put	3 @ 17.00		Significant profit from decay in 1 month. The Theta will increase as options approach expiration.
Adjustment 3: Hold Long and Buy Back Short. UVW has risen 10 points from original entry point			
Hold the Long	3 @ 23.90	**New BP**: $29.10 x 3 x 100 = $8730	Anticipating a drop in stock price.
Buy Back the Short	0		**Profit**: 17.00 x 3 x 100 = $5100.

Outcome: The adjustment capitalizes on full decay of the short put to 0. This yields an initial profit of $5100 from the short puts. The price of the long put has dropped to 23.90.

Risk / Reward Analysis: Remaining Risk and Possible Future Adjustments are determined by evaluating the remaining position. The Profit and Loss Graph for the remaining position is shown below.

Profit and Loss Graph after the Adjustment

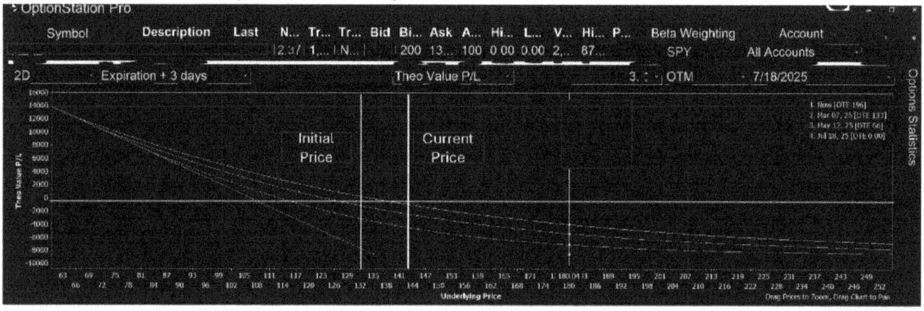

What to do Now? Possible Future Adjustments

With a profit in hand from the expired short put and now holding a long put that is 7 points OTM, the trader will benefit if the underlying stock moves down a lot. The trader may decide to hold the put for a short time watching to see what the underlying stock does. The odds are low that the stock would move enough to make the long put profitable but the trader may decide to sell the short put again and the same or higher strike price if the stock does come down some.

Example 2: Adjustment 4, Close the entire position

Scenario: **Scenario**: The underlying stock of a Calendar Spread experiences a strong bullish rally and the stock price is now at 142.

Adjustment: The trader decides to close the entire position with a profit.

Position Characteristics At the Adjustment

Position	# of Options and Price	Buying Power (BP) Needed	Why Making Investment or Adjustment
Initial Calendar Spread			
Long UVW July 18th 135 Put	3 @ 29.10	$12.10 x 3 x 100 = $3630	Slower decay than the short put, indicated by the lower Theta.
Short UVW February 21st 135 Put	3 @ 17.00		Significant profit from decay in 1 month. The Theta will increase as options approach expiration.
4.Close Position: The short leg has expired or the Underlying has risen 10 points from the original entry point.			
Sell the Long	0	**New BP**: N/A	**Loss**: $(29.10 – 23.90) x 3 x 100 = $1560
Buy Back the Short	0		**Profit**: $17 x 3 x 100 = $5100
Total Profit: $5100 - $1560 = $3540			

Outcome: The adjustment capitalizes on the decay of the short position to 0 and the smaller drop in the long-put price. The total profit would be -$1560 + $5100 = $3540.

D. Execution Plan:

Clear Action Steps: For each potential adjustment identified and ranked, develop clear, actionable steps for execution. This includes determining the optimal timing for making adjustments and any necessary preparatory actions.

Contingency Planning: Prepare for scenarios where the market moves against the position despite adjustments. This includes having predefined exit strategies or further adjustment options to mitigate losses.

Conclusion

Complex adjustments in Calendar Spreads require a deep understanding of market dynamics, a keen sense of timing, and the strategic use of options mechanics. Through careful analysis and the judicious application of advanced adjustment strategies, traders can navigate market changes, harness volatility, and steer their positions toward optimal outcomes, demonstrating the art and science of campaign trading in the options realm.

8

Adding Technical Analysis as Part of the Decision Making Process for Adjustments

---

A. Selecting Technical Analysis Tools

In the dynamic and data heavy world of options trading, particularly when navigating complex spreads, such as Batman and Calendar Spreads, integrating technical analysis into the decision-making process is vital. Technical analysis tools can offer invaluable insights into market trends, sentiment, and potential reversal points, guiding traders in timing their entries, exits, and adjustments more effectively. This section delves into selecting the right technical analysis tools to complement the strategic management of Batman and Calendar Spreads.

1. Understanding the Role of Technical Analysis

Technical analysis involves the study of past market data, primarily price and volume, to forecast future market behavior. For options traders, this analysis can highlight potential movements in the underlying stock, aiding in the timing of adjustments to optimize the spread's performance.

Key Technical Analysis Tools for Options Traders

Moving Averages (MAs): Moving averages smooth out price data to identify trends. The crossover of short-term and long-term MAs can signal trend reversals, guiding adjustments in Batman and Calendar Spreads.

Relative Strength Index (RSI): The RSI measures the magnitude of recent price changes to evaluate overbought or oversold conditions. An RSI above 70 suggests overbought conditions (potential for a downturn), while below 30 indicates oversold conditions (potential for an upturn).

Bollinger Bands: These bands adjust themselves based on market volatility, with the price tending to return to the middle band. A price move that starts at one band and approaches the other offers insights into potential market reversals.

Support and Resistance Levels: Identifying these levels can help traders anticipate where price movements may stall or reverse, critical for deciding when to adjust or exit positions.

Volume: High volume accompanying price moves indicates strength behind the move, which can be a key factor in confirming trends or reversals relevant to adjustment strategies.

2. Incorporating Technical Analysis into Adjustment Decisions

Pre-Adjustment Analysis: Before making any adjustments, use selected technical tools to assess the current market conditions. For instance, if the underlying stock is approaching a strong resistance level with declining volume, it might signal a potential reversal, prompting a proactive adjustment.

Adjustment Timing: Technical indicators can also guide the timing of adjustments. A bullish crossover in moving averages might suggest an opportune moment to roll up the short option in anticipation of continued upward momentum.

Post-Adjustment Monitoring: After adjustments, continue monitoring technical indicators to gauge the effectiveness of the strategy and be prepared for further adjustments as market conditions are revealed.

3. Practical Example: Utilizing RSI and Moving Averages

Scenario: Trader K's Batman Spread on Stock W is showing unrealized gains, but the RSI is nearing overbought territory, and the short-term MA is about to cross below the long-term MA.

Analysis: These indicators suggest that Stock W might soon experience a pullback.

Adjustment Decision: Trader K decides to roll out the short put to capture premium and protect gains, while also purchasing a protective put as a hedge against the anticipated downturn.

Outcome: The adjustments protect the position against the subsequent market correction, demonstrating the value of integrating technical analysis into the decision-making process.

Selecting and effectively applying technical analysis tools is crucial for managing Batman and Calendar Spreads in response to market dynamics. By incorporating these tools into their strategic framework, traders can enhance their decision-making process, enabling more informed and timely adjustments that align with market conditions and trading objectives. This integrated approach empowers traders to navigate the complexities of options trading with greater confidence and precision.

B. Using Selected Tools Together

Integrating technical analysis tools into the decision-making process for managing Batman and Calendar Spreads requires a cohesive approach. By using selected tools together, traders can gain a comprehensive view of market dynamics, enhancing their ability to make informed adjustments. This section explores the synergistic application of moving averages, the Relative Strength Index (RSI), Bollinger Bands, support and resistance levels, and volume analysis in concert to inform trading decisions effectively.

1. Integrating Moving Averages and RSI for Trend Analysis

Moving averages and the RSI can be used in tandem to identify potential trend reversals or continuations that could impact the performance of a complex spread.

Example Scenario: If a trader notices that the short-term moving average crosses above the long-term moving average while the RSI moves below 30 and then crosses back above, this could indicate a strong buy signal. In the context of a Calendar Spread, this might prompt the trader to stay invested to capitalize on the anticipated upward movement.

2. Combining Bollinger Bands with Volume Analysis

Bollinger Bands provide insights into market volatility and potential reversal points, which, when combined with volume analysis, can offer powerful signals for making adjustments.

Example Scenario: Should the stock's price touch or break through the lower Bollinger Band on high volume, it might suggest a reversal or significant support level. For a trader managing a Calendar Spread, this could be an opportunity to add a protective put.

3. Utilizing Support and Resistance Levels for Entry and Exit Points

Identifying support and resistance levels helps traders determine potential turning points in the market. These levels can guide the timing of adjustments and the selection of strike prices for both the long and short legs of these spreads.

Example Scenario: If the underlying stock is approaching a strong resistance level, a trader might decide to buy back the short put to capture the premium before an anticipated pullback, and / or possibly add a protective put.

4. Synergistic Use of Tools for Holistic Market Analysis

Effective use of these technical analysis tools together involves a cycle of observation, hypothesis, and action:

Observation: Regularly monitor the underlying stock using the selected tools, noting any significant signals or patterns that emerge.

Hypothesis: Based on the signals identified, formulate hypotheses regarding potential market movements and how they might affect your positions.

Action: Implement adjustments based on the collective insights gained from the technical analysis tools, choosing the strategy that aligns with the current market hypothesis and the overall trading objectives.

Using selected technical analysis tools together provides traders with a nuanced understanding of market conditions, enabling them to make more informed and strategic adjustments to their complex spreads. This integrated approach allows traders to navigate the complexities of options trading with a higher degree of precision, optimizing their strategies in alignment with evolving market dynamics.

C. Applying Technical Analysis in different Time Frames

Incorporating technical analysis into the decision-making process for Batman or Calendar Spreads requires an understanding of how different time frames can impact analysis and strategy. This approach allows traders to align their strategies with both short-term price movements and long-term market trends, optimizing adjustments for enhanced performance. This section explores the application of technical analysis across various time frames, offering strategies for effectively integrating these insights into trading decisions.

1. The Importance of Multiple Time Frame Analysis

Multiple time frame analysis involves examining the same asset under different time frames (e.g., daily, weekly, monthly) to gain a comprehensive view of market trends, momentum, and potential reversal points. This method helps traders to:

Identify Trends: Confirm the primary trend in a longer time frame and look for trade setups that align with this trend in shorter time frames.

Spot Reversals: Detect early signs of reversals or pullbacks in shorter time frames to make timely adjustments to positions.

Optimize Entries and Exits: Use shorter time frames to refine the timing of entry and exit points, including adjustments to the spread.

2. Applying Key Technical Tools Across Time Frames

Moving Averages: Utilize moving averages in multiple time frames to identify trend directions and potential crossover signals. For instance, a bullish crossover in the weekly time frame supported by a similar pattern in the daily time frame can reinforce a decision to adjust Batman or Calendar Spreads for a more aggressive stance.

RSI and Bollinger Bands: Apply these tools in shorter time frames to pinpoint overbought or oversold conditions and volatility squeezes that might precede significant price movements. These conditions can signal opportune moments for making adjustments.

Support and Resistance Levels: Determine these levels in longer time frames for a broader market perspective, then refine their application in shorter time frames to guide the timing of adjustments. Recognizing that the stock is approaching a long-term resistance level might prompt a trader to add protective puts as a hedge against a potential reversal.

Applying technical analysis across different time frames equips traders with a multidimensional view of the market, enhancing their ability to make informed adjustments to Batman and Calendar Spreads. By integrating insights from short-term movements and long-term trends, traders can more accurately time their adjustments, align strategies with market momentum, and navigate the complexities of options trading with increased confidence and strategic foresight. This approach ensures that adjustments are not only reactive to immediate market conditions but also considerate of broader market dynamics, optimizing the spread's performance across various market scenarios.

For instance, if I run a Firebird Trading Systems "DITM Calls" search tool using a 15-minute interval and find a stock that I like and want to take a position in, I would look at the stock on a 15-minute, 5-minute and 1-minute chart before entering into a deep in the money call.

D. How much credence should Technical Analysis be given in decision making

Technical analysis is a critical component of the decision-making process in options trading, especially when managing Batman and Calendar Spreads. However, the extent to which it should influence trading decisions varies among traders, depending on their trading philosophy, strategy, and specific market context.

Conclusion

Technical analysis is a potent tool in the trader's arsenal, especially for timing and making adjustments to Batman and Calendar Spreads. However, its effectiveness is maximized when used in harmony with fundamental analysis, quantitative models, and an awareness of market sentiment and news. By adopting a holistic approach that considers multiple facets of market analysis, traders can navigate complex market environments more effectively, making informed decisions that balance immediate technical signals with broader market trends and fundamentals.

9

Using the TradeStation RadarScreen to find Potentially Favorable Batman and Calendar Spreads

---

A. Introduction

In my second book, "Mastering Campaign Trading with Bull and Bear Diagonal Spreads", I introduced the concept of finding extreme skews in spreads to lend an advantage to the complex options trader. Here I repeat some of the introduction to that previous content as a framework for the discussion of finding skews for Batman and Calendar Spreads. As was mentioned in my previous book this is a great trading method with the right tools but still not the "Holy Grail". These skewed positions can be great and provide unusual opportunities, but it is important to fully analyze all aspects of these positions before jumping in.

1. How Traders Typically Look for Opening Positions

When it comes to opening positions in the options market, traders often rely on standard indicators and strategies. These might include technical analysis, fundamental analysis, and typical option metrics such as implied volatility, delta, and gamma. The traditional approach often involves identifying strong underlying assets, analyzing market trends, and then selecting options that align with predicted movements. This methodology, while effective, sometimes overlooks unique opportunities that can arise from imbalances in the market.

2. A Different Approach to Finding Great Opening Trades

While conventional methods have their merits, they can sometimes fail to capture the nuanced opportunities present in the options landscape. In this chapter I introduce a different approach focused on identifying extreme skews in the market, particularly for Batman and Calendar Spreads and new tools to support traders. By leveraging these advanced search algorithms and sophisticated analytical tools, we can pinpoint unusual but potentially highly profitable setups. This method emphasizes the importance of looking beyond surface-level indicators to uncover trades that offer high probability of success.

3. What Are Extreme Skews and Why Do They Exist?

Extreme skews in the options market occur when there is a significant imbalance between the implied volatilities of different option strikes or expiration dates. A skew can be the result of various factors, including market sentiment, supply and demand dynamics, and significant news events.

For Complex Spreads, which involve buying a long-term call and selling a shorter-term call at the same or different strike price, these skews can create opportunities where the price differences are heavily weighted in favor of the trader. Such scenarios can be exploited to set up trades with favorable risk/reward profiles and high chances of success.

4. Objectives of the Chapter

The primary objective of this chapter is to equip traders with the knowledge and tools needed to identify and capitalize on extreme skews in Batman and Calendar Spreads. We will explore the following:

Developing Search Criteria:

- How to define and implement search criteria to find Batman and Calendar Spreads with extreme skews.
- Understanding the key parameters such as implied volatility, time decay, and open interest.

Writing and Implementing Code:

- Guidance on writing EasyLanguage code to automate the search process within TradeStation.

- Testing and refining the code to ensure accurate and efficient searches.

Analyzing Search Results:

- Methods for importing, organizing, and analyzing search results in TradeStation's OptionStation.
- Generating and interpreting Profit and Loss (P&L) graphs to assess trade viability.

Practical Examples:

- Real-world examples to demonstrate the application of these strategies.
- Step-by-step walkthroughs of identifying, analyzing, and executing Batman and Calendar Spreads with extreme skews.

Note: I use AI a lot to support my code development. **Appendix C** provides an **Example of AI Support when Developing Code**.

Obviously, this is a lot to cover here in a small book, so I will not be able to cover each topic exhaustively.

B. Focus on Extreme Skews for Complex Spreads

The discussion in this chapter will be focused entirely on Batman and Calendar Spreads. The topics are applicable to all of the diagonal based spreads that I discussed in, "Mastering Campaign Trading Strategies for Complex Option Spreads", and many other strategies. The development of these topics for other complex option spreads are discussed more fully in my other books and also in the quarterly Firebird Trading Systems newsletter.

1. **Volatility Skew: Implied Volatility Differences**: In the realm of options trading, volatility skew refers to the variations in implied volatility across different strikes and expiration dates. Implied volatility is a crucial component in option pricing, reflecting the market's expectation of future volatility. When there is a significant difference in implied volatility between

options of different strikes or maturities, it creates what is known as a volatility skew. For Batman or Calendar Spreads, this skew can be exploited by purchasing long-term options with lower implied volatility and selling short-term options with higher implied volatility, potentially leading to a more profitable spread. It's kind of like ordering a cheeseburger and then finding out that the restaurant added bacon, even though you didn't ask for it.

Price Skew, Discrepancies in Option Premiums: Price skew involves discrepancies in the premiums of options with the same underlying asset but different strikes or expirations. These discrepancies can arise from various market factors, including supply and demand dynamics, investor sentiment, and external events. Identifying and understanding these price skews is essential for setting up Batman and Calendar Spreads, as they can significantly impact the potential profitability of the trade. By focusing on options where the premium differences are unusually large, traders can position themselves to benefit from the reversion to typical pricing models.

And in theory there may be no difference between Volatility Skews and Price Skews.

2. **Key Factors for Extreme Skews**

Market Conditions and Volatility: The overall market environment plays a critical role in the formation of skews. High volatility periods often lead to greater disparities in implied volatilities and option premiums. Market conditions such as earnings seasons, macroeconomic data releases, or geopolitical events can create opportunities for extreme skews. Understanding how these conditions affect option pricing is fundamental for identifying profitable Batman and Calendar Spreads. Determining the right search and filtering criteria is key to finding the type of complex spread position that you want to be in based on your anticipated future market environment.

Stock-specific News and Events: News and events specific to individual stocks can cause significant shifts in implied volatility and option premiums. Earnings announcements, product launches, regulatory changes, and corporate actions like mergers or acquisitions can lead to sharp movements in a stock's price and volatility and also create unique situations for option pricing based on anticipated take over pricing. These events can create temporary imbalances in option pricing, presenting opportunities for traders to capitalize on extreme skews in complex spreads.

Time to Expiration and Strike Prices: The relationship between the expiration dates and strike prices of options is another critical factor in the formation of skews. As options approach expiration, the impact of time decay (theta) becomes more pronounced, often leading to greater disparities in implied volatility and option premiums. Additionally, the choice of strike prices can influence the skew, with out-of-the-money and in-the-money options exhibiting different behaviors. Traders must carefully consider the time to expiration and strike price selection to effectively identify and exploit extreme skews.

Filtering for Liquidity and Volume: Liquidity and trading volume are essential considerations when searching for viable spreads. Options with low liquidity can have wider bid-ask spreads, making them more expensive to trade and harder to execute at desired prices. Filtering for options with sufficient liquidity and volume ensures that the identified spreads are practical and can be executed efficiently. Criteria such as minimum open interest and average daily trading volume should be included in the search parameters to filter out illiquid options.

By focusing on these critical aspects, this chapter aims to equip traders with the knowledge and tools necessary to identify and capitalize on extreme skews. The objective is to enhance the probability of profitability by leveraging advanced search techniques and a deep understanding of option pricing dynamics.

Setting Up Search Criteria; Defining Extreme Skew Parameters: To systematically search for Batman and Calendar Spreads with extreme skews, traders must first define the parameters that characterize these skews. This includes setting thresholds for implied volatility differences and premium discrepancies. For example, an extreme skew might be defined by a minimum implied volatility difference of 10% between the long-term and short-term options. Clearly defining these parameters is crucial for developing an effective search algorithm.

C. Developing and Implementing Search Algorithm for Stocks which may have Skews

In my previous book, “Mastering Campaign Trading with Bull and Bear Diagonal Spreads” the TradeStation Scanner was discussed and set ups and configurations for these manual searches were provided. An extensive description of these set-ups and configurations is also provided when a Skew Search Tool is purchased on the Firebird Trading Systems website at:

https://firebirdtradingsystems.com/

In this book the use of the TradeStation’s RadarScreen for continuous monitoring to find these skewed Batman and Calendar positions with help from Firebird Trading System’s indicator is described. This includes how to set up and configure your TradeStation platform to find these stocks which may have options which are exhibiting extreme skews.

Although not discussed in this book, it is possible to run searches directly with Options Data using differences in Implied Volatility, Option Prices and other important criteria, but I felt like that discussion was too advanced for this book. I plan to review that content in subsequent books. For those who are interested **Appendix D** contains information about code development in TradeStation’s Easy Language, **“Writing Effective Search Code: Introduction to EasyLanguage for TradeStation”**.

For now, if you master the search for stocks and then the analysis in OptionStation you will make great progress in mastering the selection and management of these skewed positions.

Before we dive into the details of developing searches for extreme skews in spreads lets see what Chat GPT can offer.

Prompt

Describe the best search criteria for finding a calendar spread and also describe how a trader would judge what is a good one to take a position in.

ChatGPT said:

Search Criteria for Finding a Calendar Spread

*A **calendar spread** is a strategy that profits from time decay and changes in implied volatility, using options with the same strike price but different expiration dates. The trader buys a longer-term option and sells a shorter-term option, either calls or puts. Below are the best search criteria:*

Search Criteria

1. ***Underlying Stock Characteristics**:*

- ***Stable or Range-Bound Price Movement**:*
  - *Look for stocks or ETFs with little anticipated price movement over the life of the shorter-term option.*
  - *Technical indicators such as a **low Average True Range (ATR)** or a stock trading within clear support and resistance levels can indicate range-bound behavior.*

2. ***Implied Volatility (IV)**:*

- ***Moderate Current Volatility with Expected Increase**:*
  - *A calendar spread benefits when IV rises after entry because the long option's value increases faster than the short option's.*
  - *Look for stocks with low to moderate IV relative to their historical levels. IV Rank (below 50) is a good indicator.*
- ***Low Near-Term Volatility**:*
  - *The short-term option should have relatively low IV to minimize overpayment for the premium.*

3. ***Strike Price Selection**:*

  - ***At-the-Money (ATM) Options**:*

- *Calendar spreads are most effective with ATM options because theta decay is highest at the money, maximizing profit potential.*

- *Use slightly out-of-the-money (OTM) options if expecting mild directional movement.*

4. ***Expiration Dates***:

- ***Long Option:*** *Choose an expiration 2–4 months away to allow time for movement or IV increase.*
- ***Short Option:*** *Select an expiration 1–3 weeks out to capitalize on rapid time decay (theta) near expiration.*

5. ***Liquidity***:

- *High liquidity ensures tight bid-ask spreads and ease of execution.*
- *Look for options with:*
  - *Open interest >100 contracts.*
  - *Bid-ask spread ≤ $0.10–$0.20.*

How a Trader Judges a Good Calendar Spread

1. ***Time Decay (Theta)***:

- *A good calendar spread will have a **positive net theta**, meaning the short option decays faster than the long option. This creates a profit opportunity even if the stock price remains stable.*

2. ***Implied Volatility (Vega)***:

- *A good trade will benefit from an anticipated **rise in IV** after entering the position. For example:*
  - *Before earnings announcements (IV typically rises as the event approaches).*
  - *During periods of increased market uncertainty.*

3. ***Risk-Reward Analysis:***

- *Use an options pricing calculator or trading platform to:*
  - *Analyze the maximum profit potential.*
  - *Identify the breakeven points.*
- *Look for a reward-to-risk ratio of at least* ***2:1*** *or higher.*

4. ***Break-Even Points:***

- *Evaluate how wide the breakeven range is, as it indicates the trade's tolerance for price movement. A wider range improves the chances of profitability.*

5. ***Stock Movement Assessment:***

- ***Ideal Scenario:*** *The underlying stock stays close to the strike price of the options.*
- ***Moderate Price Movement:*** *If the stock moves slightly in either direction, the strategy can still yield profits due to the long option retaining its value longer than the short option.*

Example Evaluation

- ***Stock:*** *XYZ*
- ***Price:*** *$50*
- ***Long Option:*** *Buy XYZ March 50 Call for $3.50.*
- ***Short Option:*** *Sell XYZ January 50 Call for $1.50.*
- ***Net Debit:*** *$2.00.*
- ***Profitability:***
- ***Max Profit:*** *If the stock remains at or near $50 until January expiration.*
- ***Breakeven Points:*** *Determined by the net debit ($2.00) and the behavior of the long call.*

Summary

A good calendar spread opportunity arises when:

1. The underlying stock is expected to remain stable or slightly move near the strike price.

2. Implied volatility is moderate with an anticipated rise.

3. The short option has accelerated time decay relative to the long option.

Traders should prioritize liquidity and evaluate potential profit vs. risk using tools or models. Adjust strike prices and expirations based on market conditions and volatility outlook.

Using the Firebird Trading System search tools is easy. Below the steps for running these searches in a TradeStation RadarScreen and the subsequent analysis needed are shown.

Set Up Your TradeStation Platform for Continuous Monitoring for Skewed Positions

1. **Open TradeStation RadarScreen:**

- Go to the "New Applications" menu and select "RadarScreen."

2. **Populate the Blank RadarScreen**

- Use the Scanner to select the stock list that you want to monitor.
- Copy and paste the listing, once generated, into the Radar Screen.

3. **Configure RadarScreen:**

- Then use the path "Studies→Edit Studies→All Studies" to determine the columns that you want in your Radar Screen. Suggested configurations are provided below.
- Add the Skew Search Indicators that have been downloaded from the Firebird Trade Station website. This is one that I use which includes the Skewed Search Indicators.

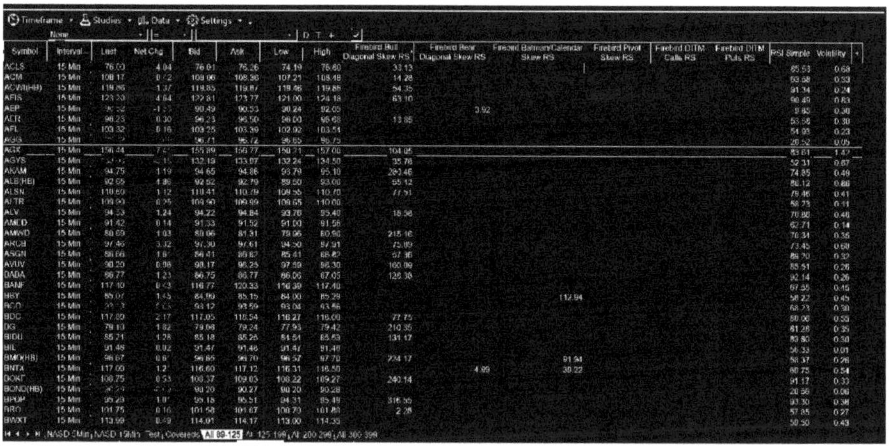

4. **Sort for Each Column:**

- Click on each column heading to sort by the highest score. These search tools are designed so that the highest scores yield the best probability of finding potential spreads to evaluate. In the screenshot below, I have search on the Batman/Calendar Skew search column. This is a snapshot in time of the opportunities identified.

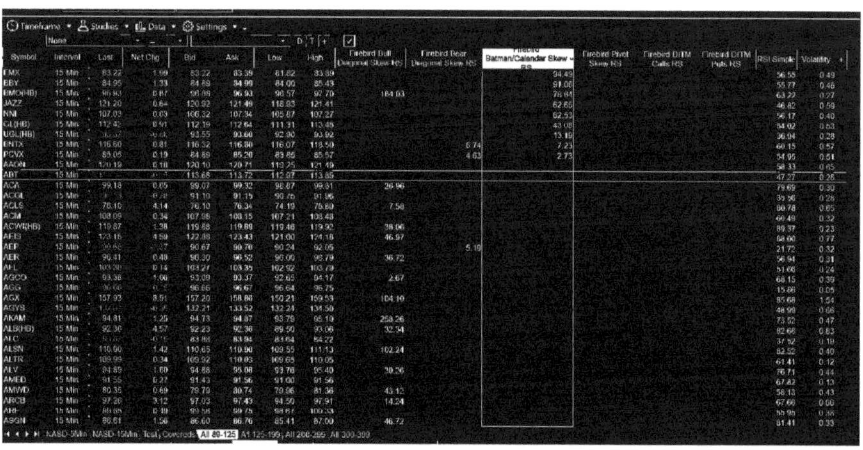

- Once the column that you are interested in is sorted select the stock that you want to evaluate and enter the symbol into the TradeStation OptionStation "Option" tab.

Analyze in TradeStation's OptionStation

1. **Open OptionStation:**

- Go to the "Apps" menu and select "OptionStation".

2. **Import Search Results:**

- Select a Stock that was shown in the RadarScreen results and select the spread type (Single, Calendar, Diagonal, etc.) For Batman Spreads use the Iron Condor category to start and modify the position.
- Select the legs and set up the position for analysis.

3. **Use the Analysis Tab to determine the viability of your selected position:**

- The Analysis Tab will show the Profit and Loss (P&L) graph for selected position.
- Interpret the P&L graphs to identify high-probability trades with favorable risk/reward profiles.

The screenshot below shows the P&L for a Batman where the stock was identified in a RadarScreen continuous search. Notice that the long options have lower Implied Volatilities than their paired short options.

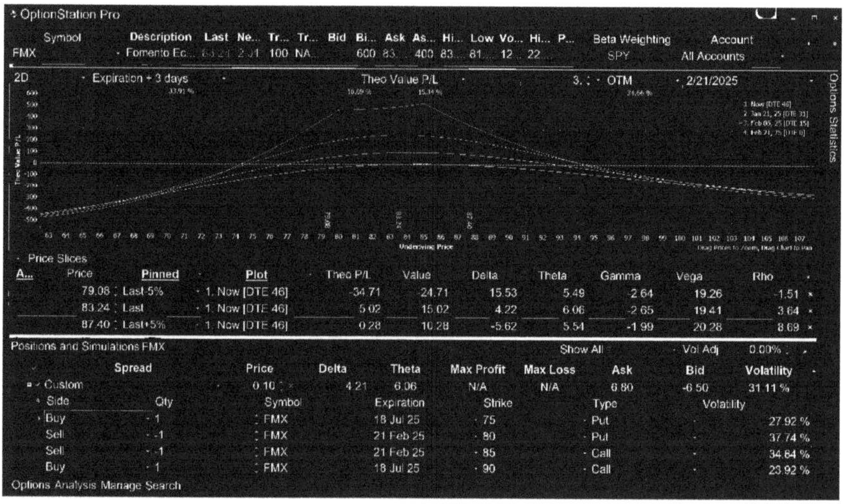

By following this step-by-step guide, you can set up TradeStation to continuously monitor for these Skewed Spreads. This setup allows you to identify high-probability trades and analyze them in detail, ultimately aiding in making informed trading decisions.

D. Practical Example: Case Study Analysis

The examples used in Chapters 2, 4, 5, 6 and 7 for Batman and Calendar Spreads were found using these Skewed Search tools and the configurations described above. In all of these positions the Implied Volatility of the Short Legs is Higher than the Implied Volatility of their paired Long Legs.

Lets look again at the Batman for the HR/Payroll Software Company. Remember that our expectation is that this stock will remain direction neutral and range bound for a period of time.

Underlying Stock: ABC, currently trading at $200.

Long Option: Buys 2 ea. 7-month out put options with a strike price of $180 (OTM) for a premium of $12.00 and

Buys 2 ea. 7-month out call options with a strike price of $220 (OTM) for a premium of $16.20.

Short Option: Sells 2 ea. 6-weeks out put options with a strike price of $190 (OTM) for a premium of $7.20 and

Sells 2 ea. 6-weeks out call options with a strike price of $210 (OTM) for a premium of $7.10.

Rationale: The long put is chosen OTM to benefit from less time decay, and the short put is ATM to generate income.

Profit and Loss Graph for this Position

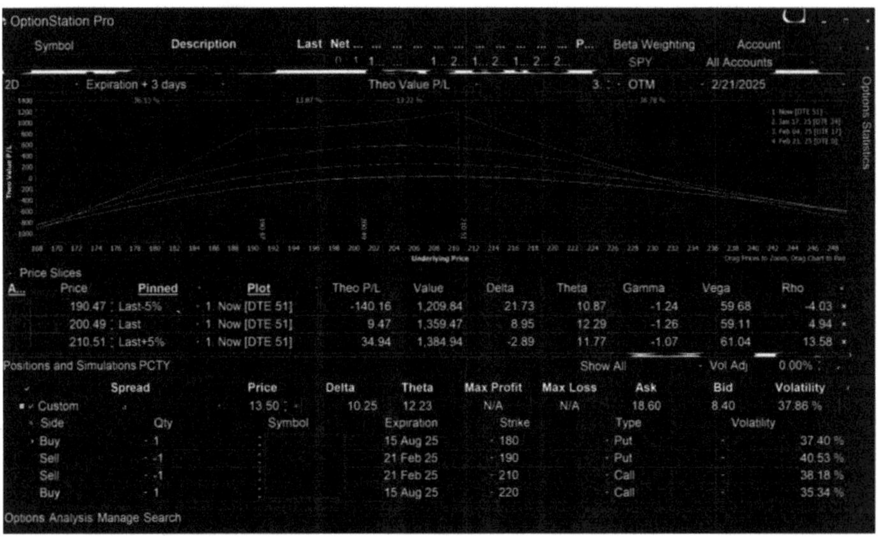

The Long Put has an Implied Volatility of 37.40% and the paired Short Put has an IV of 40.53%. The Long Call has an IV of 35.34% and the paired Short IV is 38.16%.

Conclusion

It is possible to find Batman and Calendar Spreads which offer significant advantages to the trader, but they require a detailed analysis to make sure that all risks are clearly defined before entering a position.

Traders can easily use the TradeStation RadarScreen to continuously search to find stocks which may have options with these skew characteristics. They can then perform analysis of selected potions with the OptionStation Analysis tab, develop a Profit and Loss graph for analysis.

Once positions are entered the rules and logic for determining the best adjustments to make based on the movement of the underlying stocks still apply as described in earlier chapters.

I typically maintain about 80% of my portfolio of positions using the standard method for finding positions and use the extreme skew searches for the other 20%.

10

Final Thoughts Concerning Batman and Calendar Spread Trading

A. Integration of Decision-Making Processes

In the sophisticated realm of complex spread trading, the culmination of effective strategy execution lies in the seamless integration of various decision-making processes. This final chapter synthesizes the methodologies, tools, and analytical techniques explored throughout this eBook, illustrating how they converge to form a cohesive strategy. The objective is to empower traders with a holistic approach that leverages technical analysis, advanced analytics, and market insights to navigate the complexities of options trading confidently.

1. The Holistic Decision-Making Framework

Combining Analytical Methods: Effective trading decisions arise from the balanced integration of technical analysis, fundamental analysis, and quantitative methods. For instance, a trader might use technical analysis to identify optimal entry and exit points, fundamental analysis to understand the underlying asset's intrinsic value and market conditions, and quantitative models like risk analysis and choice optimization to assess risk and probability of various outcomes.

Utilizing Decision Trees and Profit and Loss Diagram: Decision trees provide a visual framework for mapping out potential strategies and their outcomes, allowing traders to plan adjustments in advance. Risk analysis complements this by offering an at-a-glance view of risk/reward profiles across different strikes and expirations, aiding in the selection of the most advantageous positions.

Incorporating Market Sentiment and News: Staying informed about current events and market sentiment is crucial. This real-time information should be integrated with the analytical findings from technical and fundamental analysis to adjust strategies promptly in response to new developments.

Calculating Profit, Buying Power and Risks: To understand quantitively where he stands concerning any position and possible adjustments the trader must make these calculations.

2. The Dynamic and Personal Nature of Decision Making

The integrated decision-making process is dynamic, requiring constant reevaluation and adjustment in response to market feedback. This iterative approach enables traders to remain flexible and responsive, optimizing their Batman and Calendar Spreads for changing market conditions and maximizing potential returns.

Mastering the art of Batman and Calendar Spread trading demands more than just an understanding of options mechanics; it requires a comprehensive decision-making framework that integrates technical analysis, fundamental insights, and advanced analytics. By adopting a holistic approach to strategy development and adjustment, traders can navigate the options market with greater confidence, adaptability, and strategic acumen, positioning themselves for success in the complex and rewarding world of options trading.

Your Current Situation

Better Trade: Sometimes you just see a better trade than the one that you are currently trading. If you are at a profit, it may make sense to take the profit and move into the better trade.

Low Buying Power: If you are assigned on any position this can reduce your buying power. There are many other reasons that your buying power could be reduced below your comfort level. It is best to stay liquid and not get too stretched on buying power, especially in a market environment where you feel that the market could move against your current portfolio. In these cases, it may make sense to close positions that are at a profit to raise funds.

Become very risk averse: When inflation began to raise its ugly head at the end of 2021, I felt that being in the market was not the best place for my somewhat meager funds. So, I cashed out almost all and moved to a different type of investment. Sometimes you may just feel that the anticipated market is too uncertain for you to trade. Under this condition it is best to move to cash or some other type of asset.

B. Continuous learning and adaptation in options trading

The landscape of options trading, particularly for sophisticated strategies like Batman and Calendar Spreads, is perpetually evolving. Success in this field does not solely rest on the mastery of technical skills or the application of advanced analytics but also hinges significantly on the trader's commitment to continuous learning and adaptation. This section underscores the importance of an ongoing educational journey and the ability to pivot strategies in response to new information and market shifts.

1. The Imperative of Continuous Learning

Market Dynamics: Financial markets are influenced by a myriad of factors including economic indicators, corporate earnings, geopolitical events, and technological advancements. Staying abreast of these changes requires a commitment to continual learning.

Evolution of Tools and Techniques: The development of new analytical tools and trading technologies offers opportunities to enhance decision-making processes. Keeping up to date with these advancements enables traders to refine their strategies and maintain a competitive edge.

Diverse Perspectives: Engaging with the broader trading community through forums, webinars, and conferences exposes traders to a variety of perspectives and strategies, fostering a deeper understanding of market psychology and dynamics.

2. Strategies for Effective Learning and Adaptation

Structured Education: Dedicate time to both structured learning, such as courses and webinars, and self-directed study, such as reading market analyses and trading books. Focus on areas that complement your trading strategy and fill gaps in your knowledge.

Real-Time Application: Apply new knowledge in real-time trading scenarios, starting with small, manageable positions. This hands-on approach helps solidify learning through practical experience.

Review and Reflect: Regularly review your trading decisions and outcomes, identifying both successes and areas for improvement. Reflecting on these experiences is crucial for internalizing lessons learned and adapting strategies.

Mentorship and Community Engagement: Seek mentorship from experienced traders and participate in trading communities. These relationships can provide valuable insights, feedback, and support.

Continuous learning and the willingness to adapt strategies in response to new information and market conditions are fundamental to long-term success. By embracing an ethos of perpetual education, reflection, and adaptation, traders can navigate the intricacies of Batman and Calendar Spreads with greater confidence and acumen, positioning themselves for sustained achievement in the ever-evolving options market.

C. Resources for further education and analytical tools

1. Resources for Further Education and Analytical Tools

The journey of mastering spread trading, and options trading more broadly, is continuous, with education and the use of sophisticated analytical tools playing a crucial role. This section provides a guide to resources for further education and tools that can enhance your trading strategies, analytics, and decision-making processes.

Educational Resources

Books:

"Options as a Strategic Investment" by Lawrence G. McMillan offers comprehensive coverage of various options strategies, including those pertinent to complex spreads.

"Trading Options Greeks: How Time, Volatility, and Other Pricing Factors Drive Profits" by Dan Passarelli dives into the importance of the Greeks in options trading strategies.

Online Courses and Webinars:

CBOE Options Institute: Offers a range of free and paid courses and webinars for traders at all levels, covering basics to advanced strategies and market analysis techniques.

Forums and Trading Communities:

Reddit (r/options, r/investing): Engage with a community of traders to share strategies, experiences, and advice.

Elite Trader: A forum that provides a platform for discussions on trading software, strategies, and experiences with trading spreads and other options strategies.

2. Analytical Tools and Standalone Analytical Software

Brokerage Platforms: Many brokers offer advanced trading platforms that include built-in tools for technical analysis and probability analysis of stock price movements. Examples include ThinkorSwim by TD Ameritrade and Interactive Brokers' Trader Workstation.

TradeStation: Known for its advanced analysis capabilities, including strategy back testing and automation.

OptionVue: Offers detailed options analysis and modeling, including visual representations like profit/loss graphs and volatility studies.

Free and Open-Source Tools:

QuantLib: A free/open-source library for quantitative finance, useful for more technical traders interested in custom simulations and analysis.

TradingView: Provides free charting tools and a community for traders to share their technical analysis and insights.

3. Continuous Learning Platforms

Podcasts and YouTube Channels: There are numerous financial and trading-related podcasts and YouTube channels that offer insights into market trends, interviews with professional traders, and tutorials on specific strategies, including complex spreads.

D. Adaptation and Resilience

Perhaps the most crucial lesson in mastering campaign trading is the importance of adaptation and resilience. The markets will inevitably present challenges—unexpected volatility, shifts in trends, economic downturns. The capacity to adapt strategies in response to these challenges, guided by a comprehensive analytical framework and a deep market understanding, distinguishes the successful trader. Resilience, the ability to withstand setbacks and learn from them, ensures traders can persist on the path to mastery, refining their approaches with each experience.

Final Thoughts

Mastering campaign trading is an ongoing process of learning, analysis, and strategic evolution. By embracing the principles outlined in this eBook, traders can approach complex spreads with confidence, equipped with the knowledge and tools to navigate the complexities of the options market. The journey is continuous, with each trade offering a new opportunity to apply learned strategies, assess outcomes, and refine approaches. In the pursuit of mastery, the most enduring qualities a trader can possess are resilience, adaptability, and an insatiable quest for knowledge.

Thank You for Reading my Book,

Tom

Appendix A

Firebird Trading Systems Products

Option Skew Search tools

https://firebirdtradingsystems.com/scanner-tools/

Stock Algo Trading Systems

https://firebirdtradingsystems.com/stock-algo-trading-systems/

Futures Algo Trading Systems

https://firebirdtradingsystems.com/futures-algo-trading-systems/

Forex Algo Trading Systems

https://firebirdtradingsystems.com/forex-algo-trading-systems/

Cryptocurrency ETF Algo Trading Systems

https://firebirdtradingsystems.com/crypto-etf-trading-systems/

Appendix B

Glossary of Option Trading Terms

A comprehensive list of option trading terms, including the Greeks, components of the Black-Scholes option valuation formula, security types with options, and types of options, each accompanied by a short description:

The Greeks

Delta: Measures the rate of change of the option's price relative to a one-unit change in the price of the underlying asset.

Gamma: Represents the rate of change in Delta for a one-unit change in the price of the underlying asset.

Theta: Indicates the rate of decline in the value of an option due to the passage of time.

Vega: Measures the sensitivity of the option's price to changes in the volatility of the underlying asset.

Rho: Represents the rate of change of the option's price relative to a change in the risk-free interest rate.

Black-Scholes Option Valuation Formula

The Black-Scholes equation, also known as the Black-Scholes-Merton model, is a fundamental concept in financial mathematics used for pricing European-style options. The model provides a theoretical estimate of the price of European-style options and is widely used in the financial industry.

The Black-Scholes model assumes that the price of the underlying asset follows a lognormal distribution and that the markets are frictionless (no transaction costs or taxes, and the ability to borrow and lend money at the risk-free rate). It also assumes no dividends are paid out to the underlying asset during the life of the option. Despite its simplifying assumptions, the Black-Scholes model remains one of the most important tools in financial option pricing.

Spot Price (S): The current price of the underlying asset.

Strike Price (K): The price at which the option holder can buy (call) or sell (put) the underlying asset.

Time to Expiration (T): The time remaining until the option's expiration date, usually in years.

Volatility (σ): The annualized standard deviation of the underlying asset's returns, representing its price variability.

Risk-Free Rate (r): The interest rate of a risk-free investment, typically a government bond, over the option's life.

Dividends (q): For assets that pay dividends, this represents the dividend yield, which can affect the option's price.

Security Types with Options

Equity Options: Options on individual stocks or equity indices.

Futures Options: Options on futures contracts, allowing for the buying or selling of a futures contract at a set price.

Currency Options: Options on foreign exchange rates, allowing traders to hedge or speculate on currency movements.

Interest Rate Options: Options on interest rates, such as those for government bonds or interest rate swaps.

Commodity Options: Options on physical goods like gold, oil, or agricultural products.

Types of Options

Call Option: Gives the holder the right, but not the obligation, to buy the underlying asset at a specified price within a specified time period.

Put Option: Gives the holder the right, but not the obligation, to sell the underlying asset at a specified price within a specified time period.

American Option: Can be exercised at any time before expiration.

European Option: Can only be exercised at the expiration date.

Binary Option: Pays a fixed amount or nothing at all, based on whether a condition is met at expiration.

Exotic Option: Any option with a complex structure or payoff, such as Asian, barrier, or lookback options.

This list covers the fundamental concepts and terminologies in option trading, providing a solid foundation for understanding and navigating the options market.

Trader Type Definitions

Day Trader. A day trader engages in buying and selling financial instruments within the same trading day. Such traders capitalize on short-term market fluctuations, closing out all positions before the market closes to avoid unmanaged risk from overnight price changes. Day traders typically use leverage and short-term trading strategies to profit from small price movements in highly liquid stocks or currencies.

Swing Trader. Swing traders hold positions for several days to weeks to capture price movements or "swings" in the market. They typically look for opportunities where they can identify a clear price movement and then enter and exit their trades based on anticipated market trends. Unlike day traders, swing traders are less concerned with short-term market fluctuations and more focused on capturing larger movements over days or weeks.

Appendix C

Example of AI Support when Developing Code

I used this prompt and ChatGPT Response to help me get started when developing a search code for Bull Diagonal Spreads with favorable skews. AI may not get it perfect every time, but it can help you start.

Prompt

Please provide a detailed example of a Bull Diagonal Spread search code?

Response with ChatGPT

Sure! Below is a detailed example of a Bull Diagonal Spread search code using TradeStation's EasyLanguage. This code is designed to search for Bull Diagonal Spreads with extreme skews, taking into consideration the implied volatility, time decay, and other relevant factors.

EasyLanguage Code for Bull Diagonal Spread Search

easyLanguage

Copy code

// EasyLanguage Script for Searching Bull Diagonal Spreads with Extreme Skews

// Define input parameters for the search

Inputs:

```
MinImpliedVolatility(30),      // Minimum implied volatility
MaxImpliedVolatility(80),      // Maximum implied volatility
MinDaysToExpiration(30),       // Minimum days to expiration
MaxDaysToExpiration(60),       // Maximum days to expiration
```

```
    MinOpenInterest(100),         // Minimum open interest
    MaxSpreadWidth(5);            // Maximum spread width in dollars
// Variables to hold search results
Vars:
    CurrentStockSymbol(""),
    NearTermOptionSymbol(""),
    LongTermOptionSymbol(""),
    NearTermIV(0),
    LongTermIV(0),
    IVSkew(0),
    SpreadWidth(0),
    ProbabilityOfProfit(0),
    IsValidSpread(False);
// Loop through the list of stock symbols
For Each CurrentStockSymbol In StockSymbols Begin

    // Loop through options to find suitable near-term call options
    For Each NearTermOptionSymbol In OptionSymbols[CurrentStockSymbol, MinDaysToExpiration, MaxDaysToExpiration, "CALL"] Begin

        // Get implied volatility and open interest for the near-term option
        NearTermIV = ImpliedVolatility[NearsTermOptionSymbol];
        NearTermOpenInterest = OpenInterest[NearTermOptionSymbol];
```

// Check if the near-term option meets the criteria

If NearTermIV >= MinImpliedVolatility And NearTermIV <= MaxImpliedVolatility And NearTermOpenInterest >= MinOpenInterest Then Begin

// Loop through options to find suitable long-term call options

For Each LongTermOptionSymbol In OptionSymbols[CurrentStockSymbol, MaxDaysToExpiration + 30, MaxDaysToExpiration + 90, "CALL"] Begin

// Get implied volatility and open interest for the long-term option

LongTermIV = ImpliedVolatility[LongTermOptionSymbol];

LongTermOpenInterest = OpenInterest[LongTermOptionSymbol];

// Calculate the skew and spread width

IVSkew = LongTermIV - NearTermIV;

SpreadWidth = Abs(StrikePrice[LongTermOptionSymbol] - StrikePrice[NearTermOptionSymbol]);

// Check if the long-term option meets the criteria

If LongTermIV >= MinImpliedVolatility And LongTermIV <= MaxImpliedVolatility And LongTermOpenInterest >= MinOpenInterest And SpreadWidth <= MaxSpreadWidth Then Begin

```
        // Calculate the probability of profit based on the skew
        ProbabilityOfProfit =
CalculateProbabilityOfProfit(IVSkew, NearTermIV, LongTermIV);

        // Check if the spread is valid and has a high probability of
profit
        If ProbabilityOfProfit >= 0.7 Then Begin
          IsValidSpread = True;
        End;

        // If a valid spread is found, store the results
        If IsValidSpread Then Begin
          Print("Stock Symbol: ", CurrentStockSymbol);
          Print("Near-Term Option: ", NearTermOptionSymbol);
          Print("Long-Term Option: ", LongTermOptionSymbol);
          Print("Near-Term IV: ", NearTermIV:1:2);
          Print("Long-Term IV: ", LongTermIV:1:2);
          Print("IV Skew: ", IVSkew:1:2);
          Print("Spread Width: ", SpreadWidth:1:2);
          Print("Probability of Profit: ", ProbabilityOfProfit:1:2);
        End;
      End;
    End;
  End;
End;
```

```
End;

// Function to calculate the probability of profit based on IV skew

Function CalculateProbabilityOfProfit(IVSkew, NearTermIV, LongTermIV) Begin

    // Implement your own logic to calculate the probability of profit based on the skew

    // This is a placeholder example

    Return (IVSkew / (NearTermIV + LongTermIV)) * 0.5 + 0.5;

End;
```

Explanation of the Code

1. ***Input Parameters:***

- *MinImpliedVolatility, MaxImpliedVolatility: Define the range for implied volatility.*
- *MinDaysToExpiration, MaxDaysToExpiration: Define the range for days to expiration.*
- *MinOpenInterest: Define the minimum open interest for options.*
- *MaxSpreadWidth: Define the maximum spread width in dollars.*

2. ***Variables:***

- *CurrentStockSymbol, NearTermOptionSymbol, LongTermOptionSymbol: Hold the symbols for the current stock and options.*
- *NearTermIV, LongTermIV: Hold the implied volatilities for near-term and long-term options.*
- *IVSkew: Calculate the skew between long-term and near-term implied volatilities.*
- *SpreadWidth: Calculate the width of the spread.*
- *ProbabilityOfProfit: Calculate the probability of profit based on the skew.*
- *IsValidSpread: Flag to indicate if a valid spread is found.*

3. ***Search Logic:***

- *Loop through the list of stock symbols.*
- *For each stock, loop through the near-term and long-term call options.*
- *Check if the options meet the criteria for implied volatility, open interest, and spread width.*
- *Calculate the skew and probability of profit.*
- *If a valid spread with a high probability of profit is found, print the results.*

4. ***Function to Calculate Probability of Profit:***

- *A placeholder function that calculates the probability of profit based on the skew and implied volatilities. This function can be customized with more sophisticated logic.*

This code provides a basic framework for searching Bull Diagonal Spreads with extreme skews using TradeStation's EasyLanguage. It can be further refined and optimized based on specific trading strategies and market conditions.

Appendix D

Writing Effective Search Code: Introduction to EasyLanguage for TradeStation

EasyLanguage is the proprietary programming language used by TradeStation for creating custom trading strategies, indicators, and search algorithms. It is designed to be accessible for traders, with a syntax that is straightforward and easy to understand. EasyLanguage allows traders to automate complex trading strategies and perform detailed market scans to identify potential opportunities.

A. Core Functions and Syntax for Search Algorithms

1. EasyLanguage provides a range of functions and syntax structures that are essential for writing effective search algorithms. Key elements include:

- **Variables and Inputs:** Define and initialize variables to store data points such as implied volatility, strike prices, and expiration dates.
- **Loops and Conditionals:** Use loops to iterate through options data and conditionals to filter out non-qualifying options.
- **Mathematical Functions:** Calculate differences in implied volatility and option premiums to identify skews.
- **Output Functions:** Display or store results that meet the specified criteria.

A. **Debugging Tips and Common Issues**

- **Syntax Errors:** Ensure all variables are correctly initialized and that the syntax follows EasyLanguage rules.
- **Logical Errors:** Verify that the logical flow of the program is correct, especially the conditionals and loops.

- **Data Accuracy:** Check that the data being used (implied volatility, strike prices, etc.) is accurate and up to date.

B. **Ensuring Accuracy and Efficiency in Searches**

- **Optimization:** Refine the search criteria to balance thoroughness with performance.
- **Validation:** Test the algorithm with historical data to validate its accuracy and effectiveness.

B. Practical Use and Analysis of Search Results

1. Importing and Analyzing Data in OptionStation

Transferring Search Results for Analysis

Once you have executed your search algorithm for your Batman or Calendar Spread with extreme skews, the next step is to import these results into TradeStation's OptionStation for further analysis. Here's how to do it:

a. **Export Search Results:**

- After running your search algorithm, export the results by selecting the appropriate option in the TradeStation Scanner.
- Save the results in a format compatible with OptionStation, such as CSV.

b. Import Data to OptionStation:

- Open OptionStation and select "Import Data."
- Choose the file containing your search results and follow the prompts to import it.
- Ensure that all relevant data fields (e.g., stock symbol, option symbols, implied volatilities, strike prices, expiration dates) are correctly mapped during the import process.

PLEASE READ

TradeStation is making a special offer to those who buy this book.

Follow this QR Code to the TradeStation Offer page.

Scan me!

We hope that you enjoy trading at TradeStation!

Firebird Trading Systems Mission Statement:

At Firebird Trading Systems, our mission is to empower traders at every level—whether you're just starting or looking to refine your skills—by providing cutting-edge, fully automated trading systems and powerful tools for stocks, futures, forex, cryptocurrencies, and options. Driven by a team of passionate developers, trainers, and support professionals, we are committed to delivering innovative solutions that enhance your trading experience, simplify and improve decision-making, and unlock new opportunities in the markets.

We believe in the power of technology to elevate trading success, and our purpose is to help new and intermediate traders confidently navigate complex markets, optimize their strategies, and achieve their financial goals. At Firebird, we don't just build tools—we build the future of trading.

Firebird Trading Systems

Empowering Traders - Elevating Success

www.ingramcontent.com/pod-product-compliance
Lightning Source LLC
LaVergne TN
LVHW050916210926
848482LV00012B/461